Educating Musicians for Sustainability

Educating Musicians for Sustainability explores the intersections of sustainability and music, investigating how sustainability affects the development and professional preparation of musicians while asking the question, 'What does sustainability have to do with music?' The volume presents a series of case studies organised according to an expanded view of the 'four pillars of sustainability', addressing cultural, environmental, economic, and social concerns. These case studies reveal a multitude of intersections, highlighting the crucial role music can play in raising awareness and overcoming the crisis of sustainability. In examining pedagogical and practical implications, aspiring musicians are encouraged to develop a broader view of the musical profession as a human endeavour, one that is intimately related to the world in which they live. *Educating Musicians for Sustainability* addresses the most pressing and serious problem of contemporary times – and seeks to inspire changes in attitudes and behaviour, for the benefit of all of humanity.

Anna Reid is Professor at The University of Sydney and current Dean, Sydney Conservatorium of Music.

Peter Petocz is Affiliate of the Sydney Conservatorium of Music, The University of Sydney.

ISME Series in Music Education
Senior Editor:
Jennie Henley
Royal Northern College of Music
Past Editors:
Dawn Bennett
Curtin University (Series Editor-in-Chief)
Margaret Barrett
University of Queensland (Senior Editor, Global Perspectives in Music Education)
Jennifer Rowley
Sydney Conservatorium of the University of Sydney (Senior Editor, Specialist Themes in Music Education)

The **ISME Global Perspectives in Music Education Series** encompasses publications that focus critical thought in a single issue and/or drive policy and practice forward through new resources, approaches, pedagogies and insights.

The **ISME Specialist Themes in Music Education Series** includes books that draw on the cutting-edge research being carried out within ISME areas and provide a site for deep critical interrogation of the issues at hand and/or resources for practitioners based on the work of ISME Commissions, Special Interest Groups, Forum and Standing Committees.

Each series offers a focused conduit through which members of ISME and their colleagues can publish scholarly and instructional work.

Proposals are welcome!

To be included in, contribute to, and/or submit a proposal, authors must be (or become) a member of the International Society for Music Education (ISME). The collaboration with the Canadian Music Educators' Association (CMEA) also encourages and enables contributions from CMEA members for inclusion in either of the two series.

For more information please refer to the guidelines at www.isme.org/isme-routledge-book-series.

ISME Global Perspectives in Music Education Series

Leadership and Musician Development in Higher Music Education
Edited by Dawn Bennett, Jennifer Rowley and Patrick Schmidt

Leadership in Pedagogy and Curriculum in Higher Music Education
Edited by Jennifer Rowley, Dawn Bennett and Patrick Schmidt

Teaching and Evaluating Music Performance at University
Beyond the Conservatory Model
Edited by John Encarnacao and Diana Blom

Musical Gentrification
Popular Music, Distinction and Social Mobility
Edited by Petter Dyndahl, Sidsel Karlsen and Ruth Wright

The Instrumental Music Teacher
Autonomy, Identity and the Portfolio Career in Music
Kerry Boyle

Difference and Division in Music Education
Edited by Alexis Anja Kallio

Creative Research in Music
Informed Practice, Innovation and Transcendence
Edited by Anna Reid, Neal Peres Da Costa and Jeanell Carrigan

Gender Issues in Scandinavian Music Education
From Stereotypes to Multiple Possibilities
Edited by Hilde Synnøve Blix, Silje Valde Onsrud and Ingeborg Lunde Vestad

Educating Musicians for Sustainability
Anna Reid and Peter Petocz

Educating Musicians for Sustainability

Anna Reid and Peter Petocz

NEW YORK AND LONDON

First published 2022
by Routledge
605 Third Avenue, New York, NY 10158

and by Routledge
2 Park Square, Milton Park, Abingdon, Oxon, OX14 4RN

Routledge is an imprint of the Taylor & Francis Group, an informa business

© 2022 Taylor & Francis

The rights of Anna Reid and Peter Petocz to be identified as authors of this work has been asserted by them in accordance with sections 77 and 78 of the Copyright, Designs and Patents Act 1988.

All rights reserved. No part of this book may be reprinted or reproduced or utilised in any form or by any electronic, mechanical, or other means, now known or hereafter invented, including photocopying and recording, or in any information storage or retrieval system, without permission in writing from the publishers.

Trademark notice: Product or corporate names may be trademarks or registered trademarks, and are used only for identification and explanation without intent to infringe.

Library of Congress Cataloging-in-Publication Data
A catalog record for this book has been requested

ISBN: 978-0-367-49121-5 (hbk)
ISBN: 978-1-032-05913-6 (pbk)
ISBN: 978-1-003-04464-2 (ebk)

DOI: 10.4324/9781003044642

Typeset in Times New Roman
by Apex CoVantage, LLC

Contents

1 Introduction   1
Music and Sustainability 1
*The Records of Music (*Yueji*) 3*
The Harmony of the Spheres 5
Tjukurpa 7
Music as Knowledge and Music as Argument 9
An Introduction to the Authors 11

2 Perspectives on Sustainability   13
Background to Sustainability 13
Culture and Sustainability 15
Models of Culture's Role in Sustainability 17
Intangible Cultural Heritage 19
Conceptions of Sustainability 20

3 Cultural Sustainability in Music   26
Introduction 26
Ethnomusicology 27
Original Ecology Folksong 29
Intangible Cultural Heritage 32
Scaling the Octave 34

4 Environmental Sustainability in Music   37
Introduction 37
Instrument Making 38
Composition 41
Touring Musicians 43
Ecomusicology 46

viii *Contents*

5 Economic Sustainability in Music — 49
Introduction 49
The Cost of Music 50
Economic Contribution of Music 53
Music Careers as Small Businesses 55
Intergenerational Equity of Music Careers 57

6 Social Sustainability in Music — 61
Introduction 61
Symphony Orchestras and Sustainability 62
Participatory Music 64
Music and Health 67
Changing Society With Music 69

7 Case Studies of Music and Sustainability — 72
Introduction 72
Early Music 73
Musical Creolisation 76
Australian Indigenous Music 79

8 Conclusion — 84
Looking Backwards – And Forwards 84
Curriculum for Music Education 85
Beginning to Learn Music for Sustainability 87
Learning Music for Sustainability at School 88
Learning Music for Sustainability at
  the Conservatorium 90
Enacting Sustainability as a Professional
  or Community Musician 92
Conclusion – Sustainability is a Central Concept
  in Music 94

References — 96
Index — 104

1 Introduction

Music and Sustainability

There are many ways of viewing sustainability. A common initial reaction when the topic is raised is to rely on the basic definition of the word itself. Sustainability involves *keeping something going* – it could be a relationship, a job, a political movement or a television series. Music and sustainability could be summarised by 'Play it again, Sam' (misquoting slightly from the 1942 film *Casablanca*). This view of sustainability is not mistaken; the meaning of the word is correctly expressed, and it can indeed apply to a wide range of situations. Nevertheless, in our current times many people would understand sustainability more specifically as a reference to any of the contemporary problems concerning the environment – over-population, diminishing natural resources, increasing pollution, rising temperatures. In this context, people may have more trouble connecting the ideas of music and sustainability. They might think of examples such as the environmental cost of international tours by popular bands.

Some people may think more broadly than concern with particular environmental problems. They may be sympathetic to the classical overview of sustainability as a way of living so that the world we leave to our children, and to their children in turn, is at least as good as the world we live in now. This idea introduces an ethical dimension for consideration, which will be explored in more detail in the following chapter. People may have more difficulty finding connections between music and sustainability using this viewpoint. Maybe they could put forward the example of banning the use of ivory for piano keys as a measure to help avoid the extinction of the world's elephant population. It seems clear that while some aspects of life for future generations will be better – for instance, access to medical advances that reduce the negative effects of disease – many other aspects will be worse, and some may be considerably worse. An exponentially growing population is utilising resources at an increasing rate, in the meantime reducing the

DOI: 10.4324/9781003044642-1

diversity of plant and animal life and polluting the environment to extreme levels. A direct result of this progression represents the most pressing and serious problem of contemporary times, the measurable change in the earth's climate that threatens to make the planet, or at least large parts of it, uninhabitable to humans.

Faced with such problems, concerted action is needed, but in order for this to occur, there is a further complication. The current resources of the earth are distributed in a highly unequal fashion, with the large part of them being used by a small proportion of wealthy countries and people (including an even smaller group of super-wealthy people). Changes in attitude and behaviour need to be led by these most privileged people and the countries in which they live. However, these people and countries have a vested interest in protecting their positions of privilege, even though ultimately all of humanity is in the same boat, and damage to or destruction of the planet will affect everyone.

Environmental concerns are not the sole focus of discussions of sustainability. The common model of 'three pillars of sustainability' identifies economic and social aspects, as well as environmental ones. More recent thinking adds the cultural aspect to the previous three, resulting in a model with four aspects of sustainability. While this is often a convenient separation, it remains the case that every aspect of sustainability, and every problem that can be identified, is related in some way to human behaviour. Environmental aspects of the earth do change without any input from humans. Sometimes this occurs on a very slow scale, such as the extended period of cooling between the 14th and 19th centuries known as the 'Little Ice Age'. Other times the change is much swifter, as in the extinction event 66 million years ago caused by an asteroid impact, which marked the end of the Cretaceous period and caused the extinction of three-quarters of the earth's species. Such changes are not usually regarded as problems of sustainability, either because they happen so slowly or because they involve no human input at all.

This book was conceived of as a series of examples or case studies of intersections between music and various aspects of sustainability. We imagined asking a musician, a music teacher, or a music student a simple question: 'What does music have to do with sustainability?' In our experience, some people are able to give eloquent replies to this question, but many others seem to be at a loss to provide an answer. The central part of this book consists of a series of examples of the relationship between particular topics in music and particular aspects of sustainability. A chapter is devoted to each aspect, starting with cultural sustainability (Chapter 3), then environmental, economic, and social sustainability (Chapters 4, 5, and 6). The examples in each of these chapters focus on a specific intersection, such as the role of musical composition in environmental sustainability, or the contribution of orchestras to social sustainability. Then, in Chapter 7, other examples investigate an area of music, such as early music, from the viewpoint of all four aspects of sustainability. Taken together, these case studies have the cumulative effect of demonstrating the large range of intersections between music and sustainability, and provide many possible answers to the original question: 'What does music have to do with sustainability?' Of course, there will be many further examples that musical readers will be able to come up with for themselves.

Supporting these case studies, Chapter 2 sets the scene by giving a background to current ideas about sustainability, a useful theoretical framework for further thinking about the contemporary problems. Chapter 8 picks up the ideas from the case studies and extends them into investigation of the pedagogical and practical implications for musicians of the relationships between music and sustainability. This first chapter presents our arguments for the broadest view that music not only has a multitude of intersections with sustainability, but that it forms a key aspect of sustainability. We believe that far from being an optional inclusion, music has a crucial role in raising awareness of sustainability, in considering aspects of sustainability, and in humanity's efforts to address and overcome the problems of sustainability. Music in particular, and art in general, provides us with a powerful way of modifying and counteracting the non-sustainable ways of living and being that have increasingly proliferated during the last hundred years.

This may seem to be an excessive claim but we believe that it can be supported. This book is an attempt to do exactly that. The argument begins with some evidence from three quite distinct and venerable cultures: Ancient China, Ancient Greece, and Indigenous Australia.

The Records of Music (*Yueji*)

The Confucian classic *Liji* (Records of Rites) was compiled in the 1st century BC, based on writings that were ancient at the time (and have not survived) dating back to Confucius in the 6th century BC. The ideas expounded in *Liji* are still influential over two millennia later. Chapter 19, *Yueji* (Records of Music), presents a coherent theory of music and explains the essential role of music in the smooth running of the empire. The key theme is that of harmony – starting with harmony of music, leading to harmony of society, and thence to harmony of the entire natural order. Hu (2019) points out that maintaining the precise tuning for Confucian rites and ceremonies was one of the essential duties of the Emperor of China, and summarises the

4 *Introduction*

extraordinary message of the *Yueji* in this way: 'The exactitude of musical tuning of a regime not only reflects but also affects the physical and mental health of its rulers, the state and fortune of their governance, and the well-being of their subjects' (p. 13). The five tones of a pentatonic scale were identified with the functional parts of society, from the lowest, and most important, tone *gong* to the highest tone *yu*. A (translation of a) passage early in the original (Section 1.4) explains further:

> *Gong* is the ruler, *shang* is the minister, *jue* is the people, *zhi* is the affairs, and *yu* is the things [of production]. If these five are not chaotic, then there will be no discordant music (*yin*).
>
> If the *gong* [tone] is chaotic, then the music is disorganized, [indicating that] the ruler is arrogant. If the *shang* [tone] is chaotic, then [the music] is slanted, [indicating that] the ministers are corrupt. If the *jue* [tone] is chaotic, then [the music] is depressed, [indicating that] the people are resentful. If the *zhi* [tone] is chaotic, then [the music] is mournful, [indicating that] the affairs are overburdening. If the *yu* [tone] is chaotic, then [the music] is precipitous, [indicating that] the wealth [of the state] is depleted. If these five are all chaotic, and transgress upon each other in turn, this is called *man* (dissolute) [music]. If it is like this, then the extermination and passing away of the state will occur in no time at all.
>
> (Cook, 1995, pp. 30–31)

Cook considers 'chaotic' as meaning the tones are used in the wrong role or context, leading to disharmonious music. Using an alternative interpretation, Hu considers 'chaotic' to refer to the precise tuning of the tone. Whichever interpretation is correct, the notion remains that the state of music and the state of society are bound together. As Cook (1995, p. 32) explains in his comments:

> A well-run state must function like a harmonious piece of music, in that each of its component players must work together to achieve a state of balance. If any of the players (tones) transgresses upon the others, then this will lead to an unbalanced state, or a music fraught with a certain type of discordance or excessive emotive quality. If all five transgress, to the point where they completely neglect their roles, then, just as a piece of music would completely collapse, so too would the state.

Even acknowledging that the argument is by analogy, the passage indicates the important role assigned to music in Confucian thought. The text that follows (Section 1.5) gives a historic real-life example of the connection between the state of music and the governance of state:

> The music from among the mulberries atop the Pu River is the music of a lost state. The administration was disorganized and the people dispersed. Superiors were slandered and private ends were carried out, and it could not be stopped.
>
> (Cook, 1995, p. 32)

While the statements of the *Yueji* are made about states, and later extended to the (Chinese) empire, it seems a reasonable step to apply them to human society as a whole, particularly in the context of the urgent contemporary need for wise governance world-wide to acknowledge, alleviate, and maybe solve current environmental problems such as climate change. Although the term was not in use at the time, the text was written about the connections between music and sustainability, particularly social sustainability.

The Harmony of the Spheres

In the 6th century BC in Ancient Greece, the philosopher Pythagoras of Samos (570–495 BC) expounded his views of the world based on simple whole numbers and the relationships between them, part science part mysticism. He started by noticing the fact that plucked strings produced musical notes that were in harmonious relationships if the string lengths were in simple ratios. Lengths of ratio 2:1 produced notes an octave apart, ratio 3:2 a fifth apart, ratio 4:3 a fourth apart, ratio 5:4 a major third apart, and so on. This became the basis for Pythagorean (or 'just') intonation.

But the Pythagorean doctrines extended these simple relationships to the planetary scale, with the idea that the orbits of the planets were also related by simple numbers. The universe was ordered by the same numerical proportions, and so the sound each planet produced during its revolution was in harmony with the sounds from the other planets. This is the doctrine of the Harmony of the Spheres, the idea that the planets in their orbits produce a pleasing harmony that acts like background music, usually not heard by human ears as it is so pervasive that people do not even notice it, but signifying that all was well with the universe.

A century and a half later, the Athenian philosopher Plato (428–348 BC) also expressed his conviction about the close relationship between music and governance. In the *Republic*, a dialogue between his teacher Socrates and a group of companions, discussing the characteristics of the ideal state, he has his protagonist refer to the sophist and music theorist Damon's belief that the quality of music affects the quality of the state:

> Then to sum up: This is the point to which, above all, the attention of our rulers should be directed, that music and gymnastic be preserved in their original form, and no innovation made. They must do their utmost to maintain them intact. And when any one says that mankind most regard 'The newest song which the singers have' [a reference to Homer's *Odyssey*], they will be afraid that he may be praising, not new songs, but a new kind of song; and this ought not to be praised, or conceived to be the meaning of the poet; for any musical innovation is full of danger to the whole State, and ought to be prohibited. So Damon tells me, and I can quite believe him; he says that when modes of music change, the fundamental laws of the State always change with them.
> (Republic, Book IV, 424B and C, Jowett, 2017)

Plato is describing a plan for the ordered running of society, maybe a reaction to contemporary changes in his Athenian city-state. His plan includes the conservative idea of limiting music to specific instruments, rhythms and modes – the Dorian representing the 'masculine' virtue of courage and the Phrygian, the 'feminine' virtue of discretion. A specific aim is to prevent musical innovation, seen as the precursor and even cause of social breakdown. It is likely that artists then, as now, would not have been enthusiastic about such censorship, nor supported a view that it was necessary for social harmony. Even though Plato's discussion is based on myths and images, it contains an explicit acknowledgement of the important role of music in the life of the ideal state. Personal inner harmony is reflected in social harmony of the city-state, and thence in the harmony of the cosmos (Lynch, 2020).

The notion of the Harmony of the Spheres persisted throughout medieval times and well into the European scientific revolution. The medieval scholar and cleric Isidore of Seville (560–636) expressed the belief in his 20-volume *Etymologiae*:

> And so without music no learning can be completed, for there is nothing without it. For even the universe itself is said to have been put together with a certain harmony of sounds, and the very heavens revolve under the guidance of harmony.
> (Original Latin given at https://en.wikiquote.org/wiki/Isidore_of_Seville)

A millennium later, Johannes Kepler (1571–1630) expounded its basic characteristics in his *Harmonices Mundi* in 1619. He described musical harmonies and their relation to string length using recognisably Pythagorean ideas and related them to the motions of the planets. The ratios of maximum and minimum speeds of each planet's motion related to musical intervals: Earth's 16:15 ratio represented a semitone, the circular motion of Venus produced only one tone, while Mars had the largest eccentricity in a ratio of 12:5, a minor tenth. He concluded that the universe had two basses, Saturn and Jupiter, one tenor, Mars, two altos, Venus and Earth, and one soprano, Mercury. These planets had sounded in 'perfect concord' at the beginning of time, and could do so again when they aligned correctly.

The Harmony of the Spheres is a view of the world that was current for over two millennia. Although it was based on mysticism, myth, and metaphor, rather than any established scientific fact, it described a coherent view of the heavens, Earth, and its human inhabitants that emphasised the interrelationships between them, and the essential part that music played in their smooth running. Without using the actual term, it presented an approach to social sustainability based on the pervasive role of music in tying together the harmony of humanity, society, and the world.

Tjukurpa

The Anangu people are the traditional custodians of Uluru-Kata Tjuta National Park in central Australia and their lands stretch over a large part of the Western Desert. They mostly speak Pitjantjatjara, Yankunytjatjara, and other related dialects as their first language, and English only occasionally. They are one of the Australian Indigenous groups that have collectively inhabited the continent for at least 65,000 years. Their history and culture represent a remarkable example of sustainability that has important relevance for contemporary Australia and beyond. Other Australian Aboriginal groups have similar approaches and philosophies, and there are many other parts of the world where indigenous groups have lived in harmony with their surroundings for extremely long periods of time. They can also have important lessons for the contemporary problems of sustainability.

Anangu culture is expressed in and through Tjukurpa, their traditional law, stories, and spirituality. For the Anangu, Tjukurpa is not just an abstract concept but something that has a physical existence in the land and the people, and is kept alive and strong in their daily life. The Uluru-Kata Tjuta National Park website gives more information about Tjukurpa from the Anangu viewpoint.

> The word Tjukurpa has many deep and complex meanings. It is the religious philosophy that links Anangu to the environment and our ancestors. Tjukurpa stories talk about the beginning of time when ancestral

beings first created the world. These stories contain important lessons about the land and how to survive in the desert as well as our rules for appropriate behaviour. Tjukurpa stories are also used like maps. They tell us where important places are, how to travel from one place to another, and where and when we can find water and food.

It is the traditional law that tells us how to care for one another and the land that supports us. It tells of the relationships between people, plants, animals and the physical features of the land. . . . Tjukurpa is our moral compass for daily life and our justice system. It underpins everything Anangu do.

Ceremonies play an important role in passing knowledge to the people and groups who are responsible for maintaining different sections or chapters of Tjukurpa. Knowledge is carefully passed on to people who have either inherited or earned the right to that knowledge. We remember Tjukurpa stories through inma (songs and ceremonies), stories, dances and art. Tjukurpa stories are also told through various designs and paintings, such as the dot paintings of the Western Desert.
(https://parksaustralia.gov.au/uluru/discover/culture/tjukurpa/)

Tjukurpa, and equivalent terms used by other Australian Indigenous cultures, such as Madayin for the Yolngu of north-east Arnhem land, or Kooranap for the Noongar in south-west Western Australia (Bracknell, 2017), are sometimes referred to as Dreaming or Dreamtime (though this translation suggests, wrongly, that the beliefs are unreal). The maps that are encapsulated in Tjukurpa stories are sometimes referred to as Songlines (again, a European translation). These Songlines form a sophisticated system of inter-connected cultural routes mnemonically signposted in an oral tradition of song. They constitute a visual and aural map of country, and provide vital information about practical aspects such as water and food, as well as cultural aspects. James (2013) suggests that the songs and stories of Tjukurpa are comparable to the *Iliad* and *Odyssey* of Homer in the European tradition, and the Hindu classical saga *Mahabharata*, amongst others. Two well-known examples are the Ngintaka or Perentie Lizard Songline, about theft and deceit and their consequences, and the Kungkarangkaloa or Seven Sisters Songline, about pursuit and escape and the power of family bonds. Such Songlines mark the tracks of ancestral beings and indicate the crucial role played by music in Tjukurpa.

Indeed, music is effectively a store of Indigenous knowledge, equivalent in many ways to a physical library. By knowing the songs, Indigenous people become familiar with details of country even before they have been there, and Indigenous elders relate that they hear the songs when they see the landscape. Some aspects of the songs, such as those related to water and food sources, are vital to survival, while other aspects set out the responsibilities for looking after the land. Taken as a whole, they form a beautiful oral heritage of song and story.

Higgins (2020) discusses Songlines in the context of Indigenous land title claims in the contemporary Australian legal system. She notes that performances of songs often feature in such land claims, supported by explanations from community elders. She quotes Commissioner Gray's comment that:

> Often ceremony, song, dance and design are the very title deeds to land. The ability to have a particular design painted on your body, or to paint it on someone else's body, to sing a particular song, or to perform a particular dance, is proof of entitlement to particular lands.
>
> (Higgins, 2020, p. 8)

This is one aspect of music as a repository of knowledge and a moral code that indicates to people how to look after the land and how the land can look after them. Tjukurpa provides a blueprint for sustainability based on music, ceremony, dance, and decoration. The mutual rights and obligations of belonging to a particular place represent a powerful model of sustainability, particularly in its cultural, environmental, and social aspects. This is a model that has been successfully applied over an extremely long period of time and one that is still being used currently.

Music as Knowledge and Music as Argument

Yueji, Harmony of the Spheres and Tjukurpa give three examples from quite different cultures of how music is central to life, society, and cultural well-being. Although the relationship is described in terms of analogy, metaphor, or myth, this does not diminish the basic assessment of the importance of music. All three instances concur in a belief that the quality of music and music-making affects the quality and even viability of the social context and thence the culture itself. While *Yueji* and Harmony of the Spheres are ancient ideas of historical interest, Tjukurpa represents an ancient cultural philosophy that also has a contemporary existence, forming the basis for a traditional way of living in the 21st century. In all three examples, essential connections with sustainability are apparent, particularly the cultural and social sustainability referred to in the Ancient Chinese and Ancient Greek cases, and the holistic cultural, environmental, and social view of sustainability in the Australian Indigenous example.

Beyond being a means of expression, or a source of entertainment, or even an expression of cultural belief, music can be seen to have broader roles. It can function as a repository of knowledge – both cultural and practical, as in the case of Tjukurpa. It can also represent a way of thinking that goes beyond the more common logical and scientific approaches, enabling people to access different ways of grappling with and understanding problems. An example of such thinking, focused on intellectual rather than sustainability aspects, can be found in some of the major compositions of Johann Sebastian Bach. Maddox (2017) discusses works such as the *Art of Fugue*, the *Goldberg Variations* and the *Musical Offering* as intellectual creations in which the composer is working out his thoughts through the process of composition. He points out that in these works and others Bach systematically researches the permutational possibilities inherent in single musical ideas. 'In wordless instrumental compositions such as these, as much as in his major vocal works, Bach does not simply take abstract concepts first worked out in words and illustrate them in music, he *thinks* in music' (p. 335). In such compositions, music is highlighted as a way of thinking as well as a way of communicating the outcomes of such thought in an emotionally accessible way.

Making a more explicit link to sustainability, Angeler (2016) discusses the links between the auditory art of heavy metal music, and complex adaptive systems and environmental sustainability. He highlights the ways in which various subgenres of metal music can be seen as allegories of environmental disturbances. The wildfires and torrential floods linked to climate change, for instance, can be symbolised by fast and aggressive speed metal or trash metal, while the despair and agony following such events can be portrayed by doom metal's slower tempos, low-tuned guitars, and heavy sounds. In this qualitative and allegorical way, heavy metal becomes a critical thinking model and tool to provoke people to communicate the nature of problems, raise awareness of environmental challenges, and identify public action that can lead to solutions. Musical thinking is used in the service of sustainability.

The Brazilian artist Lisa Simpson, who also goes under the title of Agente Costura (agent of sewing), provides another example of utilising music as a way of thinking and exploring. In her *Musical Sewing* performances, Simpson transforms and re-purposes discarded clothing supplied by the audience into new items of fashion. Her sewing machines, scissors, and various attachments such as bells, provide an improvisational musical aspect to the show (see, for instance, the excerpt at www.youtube.com/watch?v=a1ZQoeqvfkc). The performance provokes the audience to consider issues of over-consumption, sustainable behaviour, and the aesthetics of sustainability. Simpson has stated that '[art] is a tool to create awareness and start discussions with people, and that is perhaps one artistic strategy in the fight for environmental change' (quoted in Kindvall, 2019, p. 15).

Using Simpson's artistic practice as an example, Schröder (2018) investigates aesthetic strategies for thinking about sustainability. She suggests that 'the work of the Agente Costura also sheds light on the significance of the arts as a serious field of research and the role of the artist as a researcher as well' (p. 185).

The awareness of music as a way of thought, as well as self-expression and communication, leads to the notion of musical research, or artistic research in general. The view of music – or art in general – as a type of knowledge complementing other more traditional forms drives the current focus on the 'informed practice' aspects of artistic research and the awareness that knowledge can be obtained as a result of artistic activity such as musicking. Reid, Peres Da Costa, and Carrigan (2021) give several contemporary examples in their recent collection focusing on creative research in music in Southeast Asia. In an interesting study of musical composition as a process of research, thinking through music to arrive at new knowledge, Lim (2021) suggests that

> a crucial value of artistic research is the capacity to think things that are as yet unthought; to imagine things that don't yet exist in the world and to think things through contingent logics – thinking that is synchronistic, revelatory, divergent and left-field.
>
> (p. 114)

The discussion in this chapter has given historical instances of cultural beliefs that claim that music can be related to the well-being of the environment and then to the well-being of the human inhabitants of that environment. This relationship can be described in terms of analogy, myth, and metaphor, or as a code of living. Music can function as a store of knowledge, cultural, environmental, or social, as in the Australian Indigenous Tjukurpa songs. Making music can be used as a mode of researching and uncovering further knowledge, both in purely intellectual contexts such as Bach's great works, and also in investigating problems of sustainability. The conclusion that music – and artistic activity in general – is inextricably entwined with sustainability is supported by this discussion, further strengthened by the many examples presented in later chapters linking specific areas of music to particular aspects of sustainability.

An Introduction to the Authors

The authors of this book are both academics with many years of experience in the Australian university system. Anna has a first degree and doctorate in music; her primary instrument is the violoncello, and her doctoral thesis investigated students' and teachers' conceptions of instrumental and vocal music. Anna has long experience in tertiary music education, as well as university-wide experience in teaching and learning, research development, and academic management. For the previous six years she has been Dean of the Sydney Conservatorium of Music, part of the University of Sydney.

Peter's first degree was in mathematics and his doctorate in statistics, and he has several decades' experience as an applied statistician. He has been a serious amateur musician for many years, playing recorders. After retiring from Macquarie University's Department of Statistics, he obtained a research Master's degree in music performance, writing a thesis on heritage and sustainability in early music.

Both authors have predominantly European backgrounds. Anna was born on Darramurragal land in Sydney (Turramurra), and has British, Swedish, and Chinese forebears. Peter was born in Budapest, Hungary, grew up as a refugee in Surrey, England, moved to Australia with the rest of his family in 1970, and became an Australian citizen a few years later. Anna and Peter share a belief in the importance of education, research, music, and their intersections in addressing the social and environmental problems facing Australians, and people generally, in contemporary society.

Anna and Peter have together been researching aspects of sustainability for almost 20 years. Their model of conceptions of sustainability was first developed in the context of an interview study with university lecturers at Macquarie University (published as Reid & Petocz, 2006, though based on work started in 2002). Together, they have investigated intersections between sustainability and several academic disciplines, including art and design, mathematics and statistics, environmental studies, business, and most recently, music.

2 Perspectives on Sustainability

Background to Sustainability

In the second half of the 20th century, an increasing awareness of environmental problems caused for the most part by unchecked economic growth and a growing recognition of the finite nature of the world's resources led to the (re-)formulation of the notion of sustainability. Initially, the warnings were sounded by concerned individuals and groups, but soon the challenge was taken up by world bodies such as the United Nations (UN). The most important early example of such a global initiative was the World Commission on Environment and Development. This three-year global investigation chaired by Gro Harlem Brundtland, often referred to under her name as the Brundtland Commission, produced the report *Our Common Future* (United Nations, 1987). This wide-ranging report put forward an idea of sustainability as a general world-view in which people should try to meet their needs in such a way that it did not have a negative impact on the ability of future generations to meet their needs. The actual statement, repeated with small variations at other points in the document, was:

> Sustainable development is development that meets the needs of the present without compromising the ability of future generations to meet their own needs.
>
> (2.1, p. 41)

At this stage, the focus was squarely on the environmental aspects of sustainability, although naturally the definition included the dimension of human behaviour, as a means of looking after the environment to prevent degradation. A particular aspect of human behaviour was the over-exploitation of environmental resources in the 'developed' world and the corresponding

DOI: 10.4324/9781003044642-2

problems of poverty and lack of development in the 'undeveloped' world. The report noted that:

> The concept of sustainable development provides a framework for the integration of environment policies and development strategies – the term 'development' being used here in its broadest sense. The word is often taken to refer to the processes of economic and social change in the Third World. But the integration of environment and development is required in all countries, rich and poor.
>
> (1.48, p. 38)

This seems to be an explicit acknowledgement of the fact that sustainability involves environmental, economic, and social aspects – often referred to in later discussions as the 'three pillars of sustainability'.

One particular point is interesting: the report of the Brundtland Commission uses the term 'sustainability' often but in each case as if its meaning were obvious and uncontested – it is only 'sustainable development' that is defined, and the definition of 'sustainability' is assumed to follow from that. Here are a few instances from the report: 'No single blueprint of sustainability will be found, as economic and social systems, and ecological conditions differ widely among countries' (1.51, p. 39). 'Living standards that go beyond the basic minimum are sustainable only if consumption standards everywhere have regard for long-term sustainability' (2.5, p. 42). 'Sustainability requires a clear focus on conserving and efficiently using energy' (2.61, p. 53). 'Sustainability requires the enforcement of wider responsibilities for the impacts of decisions' (2.76, p. 56). In this, the Commission was following the political lead of previous UN statements (such as the Stockholm Declaration of 1972) to link sustainability and development in order to ensure participation from developing, as well as developed, countries.

The Brundtland approach of ignoring any difference between 'sustainability' and 'sustainable development' seems common in the literature. Some sources distinguish a role for each term: for instance, 'the organising principle of sustainability is sustainable development' (from the Wikipedia page on 'Sustainability' https://en.wikipedia.org/wiki/Sustainability); and '. . . "sustainability" is a term with a more reaching set of objectives and values [than "sustainable development"], one that can support de-growth and no growth agendas as well as growth' (Dessein, Soini, Fairclough, & Horlings, 2015, p. 23). Others are more esoteric; an 'Art and Sustainability' website stated that 'Sustainable development is a sensitizing concept: impossible to define but it creates certain sensibilities and specific characteristics of the problems at hand' (quoted in Reid & Petocz, 2005, p. 349, the original website is no longer available).

At the other extreme, the concepts of sustainability and development are seen as incompatible, and the concept of 'sustainable development' as flawed and misleading, even oxymoronic. This is the case at the Thwink website (http://thwink.org/, 2014) where an explicit definition of sustainability is given as 'sustainability is the ability to continue a defined behaviour indefinitely'. The discussion then continues by pointing out that for more practical detail the particular behaviour must be specified, and gives the following three components of the widely accepted 'three pillars of sustainability model':

Environmental sustainability is the ability to maintain rates of renewable resource harvest, pollution creation, and non-renewable resource depletion that can be continued indefinitely.
Economic sustainability is the ability to support a defined level of economic production indefinitely.
Social sustainability is the ability of a social system, such as a country, to function at a defined level of social well being indefinitely.
(www.thwink.org/sustain/glossary/Sustainability.htm)

Culture and Sustainability

These three aspects of sustainability – environmental, economic, and social – have been extended to include a fourth component, that of culture. The history of this expanded view of 'four pillars of sustainability' is traced by Duxbury and Jeannotte (2013). Cultural sustainability focuses on ideas of cultural capital, culture as creative expression, and culture as a way of life and a vehicle for sustainable values. Including cultural sustainability in the discussion opens the door to further important intersections between ideas of sustainability and the field of music, which will be developed later.

Culture itself is also a concept that can be viewed in various ways. Dessein et al. (2015, p. 21) discuss a tripartite view of 'culture as the general process of intellectual, spiritual or aesthetic development, culture as a particular way of life, whether of people, period or group, and culture as works and intellectual artistic activity'. They also consider a two-level view as 'a broad, life-style-based concept referring to all domains of human life' or 'a narrow, art-based culture referring to both the general processes of intellectual and spiritual or aesthetic development and its results'. To this they consider adding 'culture as semiotic, drawing on symbols as vehicles, arguably the broadest view of all, including as it does both intentional and unconscious behaviour'.

The particular question of 'how cultural policy/ies can contribute to sustainable development trajectories' is the focus of a recent special issue of the

International Journal of Cultural Policy (Kangas, Duxbury, & De Beukelaer, 2017, p. 129). In this special issue, Throsby (2017) proposes 'culturally sustainable development (CSD)' as a concept that parallels the better-known notion of ecologically sustainable development (ESD) that has been used to combine environmental, economic, and social aspects of the sustainable development agenda. He argues that the theoretical basis of CSD is the notion of cultural capital, the 'tangible and intangible assets which embody or give rise to cultural value in addition to whatever economic value they possess', forming 'a valued resource that has somehow to be managed, and it is this management function that can be interpreted within a sustainability framework' (p. 136). Throsby lists a series of operational principles of CSD – inter-generational equity, intra-generational equity, importance of diversity, the precautionary principle, and interconnectedness – against which achievement in CSD can be assessed. He gives several examples of current issues, such as the development of indices for human well-being (for example, the Gross National Happiness index used in Bhutan). He concludes that 'CSD is indeed a concept that has *both* theoretical substance *and* a potential application to real policy problems' (p. 144).

An opposing, 'contrarian' view is presented by Isar (2017), who argues that the notion of sustainability, including its many derivatives – environmental, economic, social, and cultural, but also terms such as 'sustainable tourism', 'sustainable consumption', 'sustainable human settlements', and even 'sustainable development' itself – has been widened to such an extent that it is essentially meaningless, and can (and is) applied to almost any situation as a 'politically correct' qualifier. In the process, it has 'become a commonly shared vulgate in the contemporary *zeitgeist*' (p. 151). The strange concept of 'debt sustainability' (as discussed in the UN Sustainable Development Goals, United Nations, 2015, e.g. point 69) would seem to support this view of the degraded nature of the term.

In the same volume, Duxbury, Kangas, and De Beukelaer (2017) critique the 'four pillars of sustainability (or sustainable development) model' by identifying different roles and inter-relationships for the components of sustainability, and particularly for the cultural component. The standard model for three components has each component (or pillar) of sustainability – environment, economy, society – playing an equal role to support the whole. While useful as a metaphor, this is somewhat unrealistic as a model in assuming the independence of the components, and has the effect of reinforcing the separation in administration and policy, necessitating value judgement about the relative importance of each component. A model with interlocking circles is often used, and has the advantage of highlighting the dependence between the components (see Figure 2.1).

Perspectives on Sustainability 17

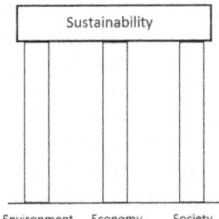 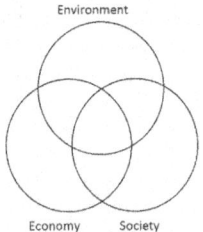 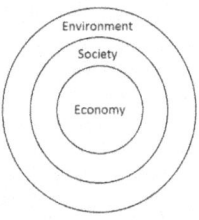

Figure 2.1 Three common models of sustainability

An alternative model for three components shows *nested* circles representing economy (inner circle), society and environment (outer circle), indicating that environmental forces constrain society and hence economy, and highlighting the primacy of environmental sustainability.

Models of Culture's Role in Sustainability

When culture is included as an aspect of sustainability, a fourth circle representing culture could be added to the last of these three-component models, nested inside environment as the second circle. Dessein et al. (2015) proposed three four-component models (see Figure 2.2), and they were investigated further by Soini and Dessein (2016): 'culture *in* sustainability' (shown as four interlocking circles, essentially the 'four-pillar model' but allowing overlap between the components), 'culture *for* sustainability' (with a central circle representing culture, intersecting with separate circles for each of the other components) and 'culture *as* sustainability' (showing culture as a large circle surrounding the three intersecting circles for the other components). These models suggest different roles for culture: as a disparate component of sustainability, as a context to mediate between the other components, or as the overall foundation for achieving the aims of sustainability. The authors write about their models: 'We suggest that this framework can work as a first systematic attempt to analyse the role of culture in sustainable development . . . used both in research and policy concerning culture and sustainability' (Dessein et al., 2015 p. 33).

The imprecision about the definition and role of culture may explain why the 2015 Sustainable Development Goals (SDGs, United Nations, 2015) made little explicit mention of cultural aspects. The SDGs were developed by the UN to succeed their earlier Millennium Development Goals as a

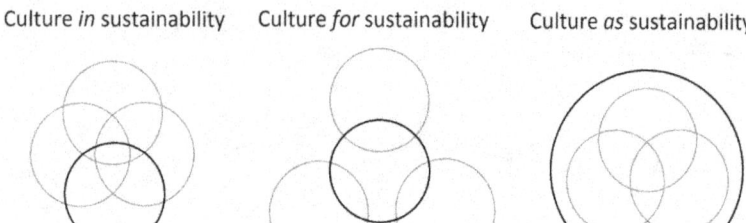

Figure 2.2 Three models of the relationship between cultural and other aspects of sustainability

Source: After Dessein et al. (2015)

framework for action. They represent the latest major statement from the world body concerning the problems of sustainability – again undefined, except implicitly as a set of visions, and for the most part discussed from the viewpoint of sustainable development. The notion of culture as a fourth pillar or component of sustainability is not evident, with the 'three-pillar model' explicitly mentioned:

> We are committed to achieving sustainable development in its three dimensions – economic, social and environmental – in a balanced and integrated manner.
>
> (para. 2)

Cultural aspects are mentioned only generally, with a specific reference to only one aspect of culture:

> We acknowledge the natural and cultural diversity of the world, and recognize that all cultures and civilizations can contribute to, and are critical enablers of, sustainable development.
>
> (para. 36)

> We recognize the growing contribution of sport to the realization of development and peace in its promotion of tolerance and respect.
>
> (para. 37)

It seems that the writers of the document subscribed to the 'culture *as* sustainability' view, of culture as a background, foundation, and enabler of all aspects of sustainable development.

Some musicians and music researchers have, nevertheless, taken up the challenge of connecting musical practice with the UN sustainability framework. The *Music as a Global Resource Compendium* (Hesser & Bartleet, 2020) describes over 100 projects showing how music can be used to address a range of human problems, each linked explicitly with one or more of the SDGs.

Intangible Cultural Heritage

Although cultural (and in particular, musical) aspects are absent from the 2015 SDGs, there is one context in which they do make an important appearance, and that is to do with the notion of intangible cultural heritage (ICH). The concept of heritage is occasionally addressed in discussions of sustainability, although for the most part the focus is on the physical aspects of heritage – historic buildings and other structures of the built environment, and key landscapes and geographical features of the natural environment. However, heritage can also include non-physical aspects – the knowledge, skills, and practices on which all aspects of culture are built, and which are passed on from generation to generation to keep culture alive. Reflecting the important cultural role of music, much of this knowledge and many of these skills and practices are musical or have musical components.

Here are some examples of ICH:

> The traditional polyphonic singing 'a tenore' of groups in Sardinia, and beyond, that dates back five millennia. It is exemplified by groups such as the Tenores di Bitti, performing songs in an improvised style. Each of the four singers has a specific role, one singing the melody, the other three harmonising with the tonic, the fifth and the octave.
>
> Argentinian tango music, and its characteristic instrumentation using the bandoneon, with strings, piano and other instruments, and the individual styles of melodic ornamentation that make each bandoneon player recognisable to the aficionados of the genre.
>
> The Brazilian Carnival festival, held in the period prior to Ash Wednesday, the beginning of Lent, the 40-day period before Easter during which Catholics traditionally abstain from eating meat, is a celebration of Afro-Brazilian culture featuring samba music and colourful processions.
>
> The tradition of handcrafting recorders based on copying extant instruments from the European Renaissance and Baroque times, particularly as exemplified by a worldwide group of master craftspeople.

Such examples broaden the long-held view of heritage as focusing purely on the physical manifestations of culture. The UNESCO (the United Nations

Educational, Scientific and Cultural Organization) page on World Heritage and Sustainable Development (UNESCO, 2018) claims that 'World Heritage may provide a platform to develop and test new approaches that demonstrate the relevance of heritage for sustainable development', although the examples given focus on the role of World Heritage properties rather than any aspects of ICH.

Conceptions of Sustainability

Next, we will describe and summarise the program of research that we have carried out with various colleagues into the ways that people think about sustainability. These investigations have been, for the most part, focused on university lecturers and students, in the context of university education in a variety of disciplines. They were carried out initially in response to calls from international bodies to recognise the importance of education in the process of sustainable development and to integrate issues of sustainability into curricula for all disciplines in order to prepare students to engage with current global problems. The report of the Johannesburg Earth Summit (United Nations, 2002), for instance, included the statement that 'education is critical for promoting sustainable development' and the recommendation to 'integrate sustainable development into educational systems at all levels of education in order to promote education as a key agent for change' (articles 116 and 121, United Nations, 2002). This research covers a time period of more than a decade, starting prior to the declaration of the UN Decade of Education for Sustainable Development (2005–2014), and includes investigations in disciplines as diverse as art and design (Reid & Petocz, 2005), mathematics and statistics (Petocz & Reid, 2003), environmental studies (Loughland, Reid, & Petocz, 2002) and business (Reid, Petocz, & Taylor, 2009) – but only recently and speculatively in the discipline of music (Petocz, Reid, & Bennett, 2014).

An early and key component of our research programme was an analysis of a series of interviews undertaken at Macquarie University, Sydney, with academics involved in teaching postgraduate students in a variety of disciplines. The study sought to discover the ways in which university lecturers understood sustainability, teaching, and the relations between them (Reid & Petocz, 2006, although the research on which this publication was based was commenced in 2002). The data comprised a series of interviews with 14 volunteer academics asking them a series of questions about their understanding of sustainability and their use of sustainability in their teaching. The participants were predominantly early-career academics from a range of disciplines – business, management and psychology; philosophy, music and literature; geology, geography and marine science, but not disciplines traditionally involved with ecological or environmental sustainability. The transcripts of these interviews (over 57,000 words) were analysed using a phenomenographic approach (Marton & Booth, 1997), exploring the range and variation in academics' understanding of the phenomenon of sustainability in the context of university teaching.

Phenomenography looks at how people experience, understand, and ascribe meaning to a specific situation or aspect of reality, or phenomenon (Marton & Booth, 1997; Bowden & Green, 2005). Marton and Booth point out that there is a relation between the way that people experience a particular situation and the way that they act in the situation:

> To make sense of how people handle problems, situations, the world, we have to understand the way in which they experience the problems, the situations, the world, that they are handling or in relation to the way they are acting. Accordingly, a capability for acting in a certain way reflects a capability of experiencing something in a certain way. The latter does not cause the former, but they are logically intertwined. You cannot act other than in relation to the world as you experience it.
> (Marton & Booth, 1997, p. 111)

This implies that finding out the different ways that people understand or experience a phenomenon such as sustainability is an essential and fundamental research step, as it is related to the various ways in which people could enact sustainability.

The outcome of a phenomenographic study is a set of logically related categories, referred to as 'conceptions' of the phenomenon. These conceptions are delineated by the qualitative differences between the categories. The conceptions and the relationships between them form the 'outcome space' for the research – a map or picture of how different people understand the phenomenon. We found that views of sustainability could be classified into three hierarchical conceptions. The narrowest conception ('distance') focused on a definitional view of sustainability as 'keeping something going'; such definitions seemed to be aimed at avoiding any further engagement with the concept. A broader conception ('resources') focused on the notion of sustainability of mineral and animal, and sometimes human, resources; it represents the more classic view of sustainability that has wide parlance in common usage. The broadest conception ('justice') focused on the idea of fairness from one generation to the next, or even fairness between groups within one generation, as an essential aspect of sustainability. Here are some brief quotations (from the original publication, using the participants' pseudonyms) that encapsulate the three conceptions:

> Distance: Sustainability just means that something can continue, that is literally all it means. Well, it just means is something going to last or

not. That's all sustainability means, and everything is either going to last or it's not going to last. Whether it is a relationship, or you know, literally it could just be a social dimension, fifty percent of marriages are sustainable in Australia (Ron).

Resources: I suppose in broad terms by sustainability I understand the idea that an awareness of resources and how one continues to produce something without using up the resources for the future. I suppose again in broad terms, things like water, energy, coal, and fuel. I suppose that's the first things that I think in terms of sustainability, natural resources which are finite, life, where you just can't keep making them (Anita).

Justice: I suppose I tend to think of it more on the environment side, so I think about environmental sustainability, in keeping the earth in a state that we can hand it down to future generations, so that it is still liveable and that there are resources that are there for future generations to use (Kenneth).

(Reid & Petocz, 2006, pp. 116–117)

As is commonly seen in phenomenographic outcome spaces, the broader conceptions include the narrower ones, so a person who holds the 'justice' view of sustainability is also aware of the 'resources' view, and can use it where necessary, as well as being able to discuss the 'distance' view. However, the inclusion does not work in the other direction: a person who holds the 'distance' view may resist discussion using the 'resources' view, and may not understand at all the ethical dimension implied in the 'justice' view.

In the context of university teaching, respondents discussed three corresponding modes of action: the narrowest approach ('disparate') encapsulated the simple idea that sustainability and teaching were completely separate activities; a broader approach ('overlapping') utilised the fact that sustainability could provide useful examples at various points of the teaching process; the broadest approach ('integrated') viewed sustainability as an essential, inseparable aspect of the teaching process. These modes of action generally, although not exclusively, occurred with the corresponding conception of sustainability – 'disparate' with 'distance', 'overlapping' with 'resources', and 'integrated' with 'justice'.

This model of 'conceptions of sustainability' has proved to be very fertile. We applied it empirically to the analysis of a further set of data obtained from interviews carried out with a group of 44 students from a business faculty (Reid et al., 2009) as part of an investigation of higher-level graduate 'dispositions'. Our thinking was that for most students, sustainability is not a disciplinary topic of study, nor a generic skill to be learnt. Rather, it represents a professional component, a core competency, that will play an increasingly important role in their working (and maybe their personal) lives. In this investigation, sustainability joined three other such graduate dispositions – ethics, creativity, and cross-cultural sensitivity – as objects of study. The approach was to ask each student about their understanding of each disposition in turn, and how it might be used in their future professional life, and then ask them to make more general connections between the dispositions. While we were prepared to identify a different range of conceptions of sustainability in this student group, as opposed to the previous group of academics, it turned out that the same model could be applied to the new group. Here are three representative quotes from the student interviews, situated in the context of their business studies or more generally; more quotes are given in the original report.

> Distance: Sustainability? Well, if I use the literal translation of the word, sustainability for, to me would mean, yeah, just longevity or something like being able to, sustainability, just being able to, you know, hang in there (Liz).
> Resources: Basically in a business/commercial sense they are referring to probably acting in the best interest of society and reflecting environmental concerns about pollution, waste disposal and scarce resources in their bottom line. . . . In an economic sense sustainability might touch on the concept of scarce resources and the interaction between demand and supply for certain resources (Kitty).
> Justice: I guess my first thoughts are towards ecological sustainability, the environment, the greenhouse effects, yeah. Just, I guess that's linking directly to, in a sense of the world that we leave behind for our children, future generations, and yeah. I think it's an important concept (Dan).
>
> (Reid et al., 2009, pp. 267–268)

It is interesting to see how similar are the ideas, and sometimes even the quotes, of the undergraduate students and the academics. We noted this feature in earlier studies of people's conceptions of environment, a possible component of sustainability. There were two groups of conceptions of environment, the first as a place, possibly including living things, maybe even humans, the second as a relationship between people and place, with place succouring people, people looking after place, or a symbiotic combination of both. Primary and secondary school children and adults showed a remarkably similar range of conceptions, although the adults tended to express them in more expansive language (Loughland, Reid, & Petocz, 2002; Petocz, Reid, & Loughland, 2003).

The model of conceptions of sustainability was also applied speculatively to investigations of the nature of sustainability in specific disciplines, such as mathematics (Petocz & Reid, 2003), and to other dispositions, such as internationalisation (Reid & Petocz, 2007). These applications relied on first linking a model of conceptions of a discipline or disposition, also obtained phenomenographically, with the model of conceptions of sustainability, and secondly, noting the tendency for the narrowest (and broadest) views of each to coexist. Thus, students or lecturers who viewed mathematics in terms of atomistic components (calculations, rules, techniques) would most likely hold a 'distance' view of sustainability. Those who viewed mathematics in terms of building and using models would tend to hold a 'resources' view of sustainability, and those who viewed mathematics as an approach to life and a way of thinking would be likely to hold a 'justice' view of sustainability. Pedagogy that helped students develop a broader view of mathematics could also encourage them towards a broader view of sustainability.

Our most recent use of the model was in the development of the 'Arts–Sustainability–Heritage' (ASH) model to 'understand the values and actions of creative workers [including musicians] in relation to cultural heritage and sustainability' (Bennett, Reid, & Petocz, 2014). The ASH model postulated views of heritage and sustainability in the context of artistic work in three levels: 'distance', where it was seen as irrelevant, 'artifacts', where it was used as a resource or inspiration, and 'justice', where it was an essential aspect of artistic work. These were paralleled by views of artistic work in the context of heritage and sustainability: 'disparate', 'overlapping' or 'integrated', using the same terms as in the teaching context. The model was then checked and validated using empirical data in the form of responses to open-ended survey questions from a sample of creative workers from the Perth region, Australia.

The model of conceptions of sustainability could apply in the same way specifically to cultural aspects, and this may be particularly relevant in the field of music. We introduced the notion of 'cultural heritage and sustainability' (Petocz et al., 2014) as an approach to the cultural aspects of sustainability (as opposed to environmental, economic or social aspects). In the context of music, we view cultural heritage and cultural sustainability as two sides of the same coin, the former looking backwards, referring to the preservation of non-tangible aspects of past society, the latter looking forwards, referring to the continuation of these non-tangible aspects into future society. We noted that:

> Cultural sustainability is based on cultural heritage, as the future is based on the past, but it in turn influences the (re-)assessment of cultural heritage, as the past is re-interpreted in terms of the future.
>
> (Petocz et al., 2014, p. 7)

Perspectives on Sustainability 25

In music in particular, heritage includes the musical legacy – forms, styles and compositions – of previous times re-interpreted, sometimes including a combination of diverse elements from different styles – a process of 'creolisation' – and presented for contemporary audiences, sometimes in the form of recordings that will survive into the future. The notion of ICH will be investigated further in Chapter 3, and the connection with the area of early music will be explored at greater length as a case study in Chapter 7.

3 Cultural Sustainability in Music

Introduction

The first case studies of intersections between music and sustainability focus on the area of cultural sustainability, despite the fact that the cultural pillar is the most recent addition to models of sustainability. In the discipline of music, intersections with cultural sustainability seem to be the most obvious and most natural ones. Historically, also, the first discussions of sustainability and music took place within the sub-discipline of ethnomusicology, in the context of investigating, safeguarding, and promoting the music of groups whose traditional culture was threatened in some way. A discussion of ethnomusicology in general forms the first case study, and this is followed by the study of a specific example, the original ecology folksong movement in contemporary China. The notion of intangible cultural heritage (ICH) was introduced at the end of the previous chapter. The third case study considers ICH in the context of UNESCO's ICH website, its lists of cultural practices collected and augmented annually, and the interactive graphics that can be used to explore the relationships between them. The final case study of the chapter investigates a specific instance of ICH, the notion of musical scale as a cultural artefact.

In terms of the framework of conceptions of sustainability, all four case studies – and other examples of cultural sustainability in music – start from a 'resources' view. The resources in these cases are cultural resources, and sustainability implies looking after these cultural resources, preserving and safeguarding them if they are threatened in some way, and making use of them in the future, as cultural products that form part of human legacy. They may even be used, in some instances, to restore or reinvigorate cultural practices that have been neglected or almost extinguished. This aspect then introduces the 'justice' view of sustainability, with the idea that cultures – including their musical aspects – have a right to continue to be expressed. According to this view, people in general, particularly members of a dominant culture, have an ethical imperative to help cultures remain viable. The ensuing diversity of cultures and cultural artefacts, including musics, is a cultural resource that benefits everyone, in much the same way that diverse ecological resources benefit humanity – sometimes in ways that are as yet unknown and unappreciated.

The case studies in this section illustrate the temporal dimension of the notions of cultural heritage and cultural sustainability that were discussed in the previous chapter. These are clearly expressed in the general investigations of ethnomusicology and of ICH, and also in the specific examples of original ecology folksong and scales. All four examples demonstrate the backward-looking view to non-tangible aspects of the cultural heritage of past societies. At the same time, they demonstrate the forward-looking view based on preserving these cultural artefacts and continuing to present them to contemporary and future society. While this temporal dimension can be seen in all aspects of sustainability, including the environmental, economic, and social aspects, it is most clearly situated in cultural sustainability where it forms an essential feature.

Ethnomusicology

Ethnomusicologists study the musical practices of particular groups of people. These could be indigenous cultural groups, often outside the common familiarity of Western countries, or they could comprise social subgroups in contemporary Western experience. This sub-discipline of music represented until recently the area that engaged most with ideas of sustainability, and particularly cultural sustainability. This can be most commonly identified using the 'resources' conception of sustainability, specifically cultural resources, with the focus on the conditions necessary for keeping the musical practices of a group of people alive and viable.

One example is that of Chan and Saidon (2017), who advocate for the traditional indigenous music known as *sewang* of the Semai people in peninsular Malaysia. They identify a threat to this music from the changing lifestyle of Semai youth, particularly their growing interest in local and international popular music. The authors' suggested solution is the development of a contemporary version of *sewang* that merges traditional elements and popular styles. This could increase the interest of local youth as well as provide practical benefits in improved tourism opportunities. In a subsequent article, Chan (2018) reports on the preparation of a resource package – four books and a recording that retell folk stories of the folk hero Bah Luj, with background music inspired by Semai music. Cultural sustainability is achieved by collaboration between culture bearers and academics, with the composed music bridging Semai traditions and an international audience.

Another example focuses on urban culture in Papua New Guinea. Wilson (2013) explores the ways in which urban popular music recorded commercially by New Guinea band Paramana Strangers helps to sustain the traditional culture of their original home. The popular songs of this band enable the preservation of important traditions of Paramana Village, some five hours drive from the capital, Port Moresby. The texts often utilise traditional environmental metaphors, such as that of the *gavurivo* afternoon sea breeze that induces a pleasant but sad feeling. They may be based on ancient texts, sung in the archaic poetic language of Old Aroma. Wilson writes from personal knowledge of the band members and his time spent in their home village. The band's contribution as co-researchers ensures that indigenous ways of knowing and imparting knowledge are given priority, including their ideas about the sustainability of their traditional culture.

Many ethnomusicological studies contain an implicit acknowledgement of the broadest conception of sustainability, the 'justice' conception, adding the ethical viewpoint that all groups have a right to conditions in which their culture can continue to thrive. This is not surprising, given a widespread definition of the field:

> Applied ethnomusicology is the approach, guided by principles of social responsibility, which extends the usual academic goal of broadening and deepening knowledge and understanding toward solving concrete problems and toward working both inside and beyond typical academic contexts.
> (International Council for Traditional Music, 2020)

In one of the papers in a *Musicology Australia* special issue on music and sustainability, Gillespie (2013) discusses the preparation of a cultural heritage plan for social stability and harmony for the Lihir people of Papua New Guinea. The island on which they live is the site of a large gold mine, bringing practical benefits such as the development of infrastructure, employment opportunities, and improved education and health care. However, there are concomitant concerns about their social landscape and their customary practices, for which the mining company has some responsibility. The cultural heritage plan addresses the future of Lihir culture and the effective governance of its society, setting out the responsibilities of all parties, including the ethnomusicologist and the mining company. Gillespie states explicitly that 'The ethnomusicologist is in a unique position to contribute to corporate social responsibility in mining, especially in the realm of intangible cultural heritage' (p. 185).

In an earlier *The World of Music* special issue on the same topic, Titon's (2009) editorial talks about music as a sustainable biocultural resource, including 'the ethical argument that all peoples and their cultures have a right to survive, even to flourish' (p. 6). This makes an explicit statement of the 'justice' view of sustainability. Indeed, Titon has for many years maintained an academic blog on music and sustainability (see https://sustainablemusic.blogspot.com/) in which he posts regular discussions about a wide range of topics, underpinned by an obvious advocacy for social justice as a key component of cultural and ecological sustainability. A post dated May 2020, for instance, discusses the sustainability of blues and careers as blues players in the context of social upheaval in Minneapolis (May 31, 2020) and an earlier post summarises his research into religious folklife in communities in Stanley, Virginia, and Detroit (July 27, 2018).

Another ethnomusicological study of religious practices that shares this justice view of sustainability is Stefano and Murphy's (2016) examination of the 'Singing and Praying Bands' living tradition. Set in the Chesapeake region of the United States (US), this tradition developed from covert religious observances of enslaved African–American people before the US Civil War. Their study is set up using a 'resources' view of sustainability, but soon becomes explicit about the 'justice' view:

> Bringing these social justice considerations [addressing inequalities, racism, etc.] into the ICH discourse spotlights the need to prioritise a sharing of authority and expertise between cultural community and heritage professional during all steps of the safeguarding process – from identification of community needs to subsequent promotional efforts.
> (p. 611)

Many more examples could be given. Ethnomusicology is an area of music that has a long tradition of engaging with aspects of sustainability, particularly with the issues of cultural sustainability.

Original Ecology Folksong

China is the most populous country in the world, with just under 1.5 billion people representing almost one-fifth of the world's population of 8 billion. For most people in the Western world, and in particular most scholars and most musicians, it is difficult to know what is happening in China beyond what is reported in the mass media – and that is limited by control from China and selection by Western media. Much of China's academic and scientific output is published only in Mandarin, so most non-Chinese are unable to understand it. Yet, what happens in China in terms of sustainability in all its aspects – environmental, economic, social, and cultural – is vitally important to the world as a whole.

Thus, it is interesting to report on an aspect of sustainability – particularly cultural but also related to ecological sustainability – that seems to represent an important development in China in the early 21st century. The notion of 'original ecology folksong' (*yuanshengtai min'ge*) has, since about 2004, been used to refer to traditional folksongs performed in native dialect and authentic rustic style by local singers. This approach is contrasted to professionally recomposed folksongs, performed in a standard style by trained singers with elaborate instrumental accompaniment, the common method of presentation in the late 20th century (Rees, 2016). A related 'original ecology' movement, applied to a whole range of products (in much the same way as 'organic' or 'ecological' is used in Western countries), seems to combine desire for cultural sustainability, particularly of music of minority groups, with growing concerns for environmental sustainability.

The background of this 'original ecology' movement can be found in the rapid economic and technological development since the Cultural Revolution of 1966–1976. The reform and openness of this period have changed the Chinese world profoundly, physically, socially, and culturally. An obvious change was a growth in the urban population at the expense of the rural; in 1990, 20% of Chinese people lived in cities, but that had risen to over 60% by 2020. China has become the world's largest manufacturing economy, and the world's largest or second-largest economy (depending on how it is measured). The standard of living, particularly for the growing predominantly urban middle class, now more than half the population, has increased steadily. Yet, these undoubted benefits have come at the expense of significant environmental degradation, cultural dislocation, and the growth of state surveillance and consequent limitations on personal freedoms, problems borne, as always, disproportionally by minorities and the poorest.

'Han' Chinese make up over 90% of the population of China, and are the majority group in every province except the Xinjiang and Tibet Autonomous Regions, which have Uyghur and Tibetan majorities respectively. China recognises 55 distinct minority groups, and the country seems to have a sometimes-ambivalent relationship with these groups. On the one hand, China is proud of the cultural diversity that they represent, highlighting their music and culture as tourist attractions and putting them forward for international recognition (such as the UNESCO lists of ICH). On the other hand, China is also worried about the 'threat' that minority groups may represent, socially, culturally, and politically, to their centralised political system, most particularly in terms of separatist movements.

Wong (2019) investigates Dolan music and Ili folk-singing, both products of Uyghur culture. He quotes from promotional material about Uyghur entries in folk music contests that such music 'assembles the primordial power of simplicity and wilderness' (p. 208) and is concerned with 'equality among humans, and peaceful relations between human beings and nature' (p. 209). An example, the folksong 'Ili Boyliri' ('Banks of the Ili river') can be viewed at www.youtube.com/watch?v=cueCkSLB_O8. The original ecology aesthetic rediscovers and embraces previously unwanted attributes – indigenous languages, untutored style, and local flavours and values. The approach keeps traditional music recognisable and relevant – and also marketable – and is a way of ensuring cultural sustainability in the current increasing censorship of Uyghur culture.

D'Evelyn (2018) investigates the original ecology movement in the music of Inner Mongolia, particularly the 'long songs' of the grasslands. Long song (*urtiin duu*) is an essential part of the Mongolian music tradition, a profound, meditative, and soulful style of singing, with philosophical, romantic, or festive themes. It is named after the elongated vocal syllables, a characteristic that is thought to reflect the vast open spaces of the steppes. A brief example can be heard at www.youtube.com/watch?v=MtAaasP3XRo – some of the longest 'majestic' songs can take several hours for a full performance. D'Evelyn discusses the singing of Lu Badma (or Badema), who was conferred as official 'cultural transmitter' of Mongolian long song in 2008. Coming from a herding background in the Alasha (Alxa) region, she sings in a variety of local styles free from any conservatory influences, often accompanying herself on the horsehead fiddle or *morin huur*, illustrating the characteristics of the original ecology folksong ethos.

The original ecology folksong movement in China represents a reassessment and revaluing of characteristics such as coarse, backward, and unscientific that have previously been applied to the musics of minority groups. Now, authentic and traditional folk-singing is being compared positively to the conservatory or national singing style, developed for large, official stage entertainment. Wong (2019, p. 218) points out that the original ecology style 'reflects an aesthetic turn that speaks less about minority performing arts but more about the shifting preferences of Chinese consumers'. Nevertheless, it comes at a time of increasing concerns for environmental degradation and loss of culture, and reflects an increasing nostalgia for their passing. Rees (2016) points out the obvious connections with the Western interest in the sustainability of traditional music and the growing field of ecomusicology. She states that:

> The concept of the original ecology folksong sums up the Zeitgeist of a nation that has only recently begun to value its myriad local cultures and take seriously the frightening degradation of its natural environment, and indeed to connect the two.
>
> (p. 76)

Intangible Cultural Heritage

UNESCO has a website for ICH (https://ich.unesco.org/en) that contains a wealth of information about the ideas and the practical aspects of it. Using this as a starting point, this section looks at the musical aspects of ICH and their relation to cultural sustainability. Under the main heading 'Convention', the text of the 2003 Convention for the Safeguarding of the Intangible Cultural Heritage (UNESCO, 2003) is given in full. This Convention defines ICH as 'the practices, representations, expressions, knowledge, skills – as well as the instruments, objects, artefacts and cultural spaces associated therewith – that communities, groups, and, in some cases, individuals recognize as part of their cultural heritage' (Article 2.1). A section entitled 'What is Intangible Cultural Heritage?' states that ICH:

> includes traditions or living expressions inherited from our ancestors and passed on to our descendants, such as oral traditions, performing arts, social practices, rituals, festive events, knowledge and practices concerning nature and the universe or the knowledge and skills to produce traditional crafts.

The discussion also points out that ICH is contemporary as well as traditional, and so includes living rural and urban practices, and that it depends on recognition from the specific communities, groups, or individuals that create, maintain, and transmit the culture.

Many of these expressions of ICH are related in some way to music, reflecting the important role of music in cultural life. Under the main heading 'Lists', UNESCO displays the cultural practices that they have inscribed into their register, linked to more detailed written and audio-visual information. These lists are created annually, and the entries from 2008 to 2019 contain 549 elements from 127 separate countries (only countries that have ratified the Convention are allowed to contribute). Some specific examples can show the range of music and music-related elements of ICH.

> Mongolian *khöömei* (inscribed in 2010) is a type of singing that uses overtones. The singer produces a fundamental pitch and uses their vocal apparatus to add further pitches, creating two, three, or even four sounds together. The extra lines can be above or below the fundamental note, and the melody is created in the top line, a high whistling, by changing the shape of the mouth and throat. The technique is traditionally transmitted orally from master to apprentice. *Khöömei* is based on the sounds of nature, the birds, the wind, and the vast open grasslands of the Mongolian plains. *Khöömei* singing is a basic expression

of Mongolian culture, used in a range of social occasions from lulling babies to sleep to grand official ceremonies.

Irish harping (inscribed in 2019) is a characteristic musical expression of the people of Ireland, and the harp has been played there for over a millennium. The musical skills are traditionally transmitted orally, although nowadays increasingly using musical notation. The most famous historical exponent of harp playing was the composer, singer and harpist Turlough O'Carolan (1670–1738), who spent almost 50 years travelling the country, composing, and playing instrumental pieces and songs. Historically, harps were strung with wire or gut, and some contemporary players keep the old repertoire and playing styles alive. A growing interest in harping and regular harp festivals attest to the instrument's important role in Irish identity and culture.

The Ethiopian Orthodox Epiphany festival of *Timkat* (inscribed in 2019) on January 18, celebrates the baptism of Jesus Christ by John the Baptist in the River Jordan. The evening before, a model of the Ark of the Covenant is wrapped in rich cloth and taken in procession to a nearby stream or pool, where people spend the night praying and singing. In the morning, the water is blessed and sprinkled on the congregation. The Ark is then returned to its usual place on the church altar, and the evening feast follows. Traditional and religious songs and music form an essential component of the whole ceremony.

A final example is the art of making and playing the *kamancha*, a bowed stringed instrument of Azerbaijan and Iran (inscribed in 2017) and an essential part of their musical culture. In these countries, the instrument is widely used in both classical and folk music, in repertoire that ranges from the mythological to comic social commentary. Many instruments are made by local craftspeople, providing them with a living and at the same time keeping the traditional heritage of their communities alive. Knowledge of making and performing on *kamancha*, and its role in promoting cultural identity, has always been transmitted orally within families, augmented now by state support at schools and musical institutions.

The front page of the UNESCO ICH website also contains some fascinating interactive graphics organising the listed cultural practices and expressions by themes (such as 'vocal music', 'festivals', or 'dance'), by biomes and natural resources (such as 'forests', 'inland wetlands', or 'urban areas'), and by threats (such as 'negative attitudes', 'economic pressure', and 'weakened practice and transmission'). A final graphic organises the practices under the five domains of the Convention. These interactive graphics allow in-depth exploration of the complete collection of the cultural practices and expressions, and the relationships between them.

While the UNESCO examples of ICH are, for the most part, in the form of traditional practices of specific, often indigenous, groups of people, the concept of ICH is broad enough to include recently created contemporary culture, practices of urban groups, and historical or hypothetical instances. Withers (2015), for example, reports on the Women's Liberation Music Archive, an online collection of photographs, film, video, and oral histories concerned with the UK Women's Liberation Movement from 1970 to 1989 (at https://womensliberationmusicarchive.co.uk/). The collection of grassroots political music documents an important social change in post-war Britain as women challenged and redefined their place within society. This alternative heritage rock project was set up by two of the original members (including the author) as an exhibition of feminist music-making that does not appear in standard histories of rock.

In another interesting instance, Suárez, Alonso, and Sendra (2015) recover the lost or forgotten ICH of the soundscape of the Romanesque cathedral in Santiago de Compostela, Spain, using a process of 'acoustic archaeology'. Their computer modelling of the cathedral as it was originally, before later extensive remodelling, allows them to make conclusions about the sounds that would have been heard by visiting pilgrims in the late 11th century. These are illustrated by audio files of choral singing as it would have sounded in the empty building, and then in the church full of worshippers.

Scaling the Octave

At its most essential, a scale is a sequence of pitches usually arranged in ascending or descending order and usually dividing an octave. However, this is only a starting point, and the concept includes a large range of diverse ideas. Gelbart (2018) points out that scale can be considered from the view of performance – as a rising or falling sequence of notes that are played (and practised) as components of melodies – or from the view of theory – as a selection of the possible pitches that could be used in a musical situation. Scale can also be viewed as a cultural artefact, a characteristic form of artistic expression of a group of people, and thus a form of ICH with an immediate connection with ideas of cultural sustainability.

Some aspects of musical scales are linked to physical reality; the physical basis of pitch is that each note is defined by the frequency at which it beats (as in the orchestral standard A440, beating at 440 Hertz or cycles per second). Since the time of Pythagoras (6th century BC) people have known that strings beating in ratios of small whole numbers produce intervals such as the octave (ratio 2:1), the fifth (3:2) and the fourth (4:3) that sound well together. And a note played on any instrument contains overtones or harmonics that beat at simple multiples of the fundamental note. The first harmonic has a ratio of 2:1 with the fundamental note, the second harmonic has a ratio of 3:2 with the first harmonic, and the third harmonic has a ratio of 4:3 with the second harmonic. These represent intervals of an octave, a fifth and a fourth, respectively.

However nice this might look numerically, there are inherent problems in 'just' intonation – using such simple ratios as the basis of intervals and scales. Using repeated intervals of a fifth will never lead to an octave relationship with the fundamental note (mathematically, repeated multiplication by 3/2 can never be equal to any repeated multiplication by 2/1). Tempering (or modifying) these just intervals can be used to obtain workable results, but the details of temperament are to some extent a psychological and cultural choice. Scales can be investigated mathematically, but mathematics is not enough to explain all their details.

From the theoretical viewpoint, it is interesting to examine possible principles of scale construction. Three ideas are particularly important: harmonicity favours intervals based on simple whole-numbered ratios, compression suggests that there should be only a few different step sizes on the scale, and transmittability requires enough gap between steps so that they can be easily distinguished. McBride and Tlusty (2020) investigate a database of 742 scales from a variety of cultures and conclude that scales relying on 'imperfect fifths' (just fifths with a tolerance for error) were most likely, and that compressible scales were also favoured. This indicates that only the first few harmonics and only step sizes of one or two units form the basis of most scales used around the world.

The standard Western scale divides the octave into 12 equal steps (semitones) and selects seven of these for use in the 'major' and the 'minor' scales. Historically, other selections of seven gave the 'modes' of early church music, and selection of all twelve semitones gives the chromatic scale, used in 20th-century 12-tone serialism, for instance. Such a scale, built on equal steps, is referred to as equal tempered. There is a long history of the modification of scales built on just fifths or thirds (ratios 3:2 or 5:4), using various 'mean tone' temperaments. The equal-tempered scale allows keyboard instruments to be played (more or less) in tune in any key, but the earlier tempered scales sound better in tune if only a few related keys are utilised.

Many scales in other cultures are also equal tempered, but divide the octave into a different number of steps. Thai and Khmer (Cambodian) traditional musics use equal-tempered scales with seven steps, the Balinese *slendro* gamelan scale is equal tempered and pentatonic, while the Javan *pelog* gamelan scale has nine equal steps of which seven are used, resulting in five small and two large intervals (compared to the Western major scale with five large and two small intervals). Ethiopian *kiñit* scales are pentatonic, like a selection of five notes from the Western equal-tempered scale, with intervals of one to four semitones; for instance, the *anchihoya* scale can be written as C-D♭-F-G♭-A-C, with intervals of 1-4-1-3-3 semitones. More complex are the 17-tone Arabic *maqam* modes, based originally on 'Pythagorean' intervals, but now usually converted to a Western quartertone scale with 24 equal steps.

Music is an expression of human culture both overall as a means of communicating artistic vison but also in terms of its components, such as scale. The vast diversity of scales used by human groups is a reflection of many different views of the ways that sounds can be put together to communicate. The Western major and minor scales are commonly associated with joyous and sad feelings respectively, and the early church modes claimed to represent different emotional states. There are suggestions that scales and tunings can in themselves be a means of expression, both personal and cultural. The just scales used by Terry Riley in his improvisatory compositions on *The Harp of New Albion* are a personal artistic expression that can be heard and felt by any listener. In European Baroque music, the mean tone temperament used by Bach in his *St Matthew Passion* reflects the agony of events in the jarring remote keys used during the betrayal and crucifixion scenes, and would have been understood by musicians and audiences of the time. The philosophical statement of Uzbek instrumentalist and composer, Turgun Alimatov, that 'a musician should first tune himself, then his instrument, and then the listener' (Matyakubov, 1993, p. 62) expresses the importance of the cultural heritage of tuning and scale.

4 Environmental Sustainability in Music

Introduction

This chapter presents four case studies of the intersections between music and sustainability in the area of environmental sustainability. This is the first of the classical 'three pillars of sustainability' and, based on interviews that the authors have undertaken in previous research projects, this is the area that most people think about first when their thoughts turn to sustainability. A discussion of musical instrument making forms the first case study. Many musical instruments use specific materials in their construction, often based on long traditions and experience of instrument making. As the required number of instruments increases, to satisfy the demand from growing numbers of musicians, some of these materials move from being rare and specialised to being endangered. Alternative materials and alternative construction methods can provide some relief, but only when musicians and makers recognise the problems. From a different viewpoint, the second case study looks at the relationship between composition and environmental sustainability. Musical compositions can utilise environmental themes and highlight environmental problems, bringing them to the attention of a greater number of people. Artistic creations can contribute to a reassessment of attitudes towards the environment and a re-imagining of alternative possibilities for human behaviour and existence.

The third case study brings to attention the environmental problems related to individual and groups of musicians touring. Such travelling has always been part of the professional life of musicians, but in the contemporary world the related resources have grown to dangerous levels. While an individual soloist visiting Australia from Europe for a performance has to consider the environmental impact of air travel from one side of the globe to the other, a visiting orchestra multiplies these effects by 50 or 100. Some popular artists and groups are even more extreme. The set and production equipment for Beyoncé's Formation World Tour, from April to

DOI: 10.4324/9781003044642-4

October 2016, filled seven Boeing-747s and required more than 70 trucks for its performances to audiences of more than two million in cities across North America and Europe. The final case study is again quite different, investigating a new sub-discipline of music, ecomusicology, that focuses on the relationships between music, or sound in general, and the environment. Since the early 2000s, ecomusicology has developed as an area of musical thinking that is particularly focused on environmental problems, a context where musicians and researchers can confront current environmental realities, and plan appropriate action.

In the area of environmental sustainability particularly, the basic approach to sustainability is from the 'resources' viewpoint. The pressure on environmental resources of all varieties, caused by increasing population growth and unthinking over-utilisation of resources, is one of the basic environmental problems of the contemporary world, leading to the major problem of climate change. It is only a small step to the 'justice' view of sustainability, recognising that diminishing resources will result in serious problems for future generations, but also that the squandering of environmental resources is being carried out by only a minority of the world's population, while the majority struggle to get access to the smallest share of them. The approach of ecomusicology puts this 'justice' viewpoint into the centre of musical consciousness, and the composition case study highlights the idea that musical ideas and creations can change people's attitudes and behaviours to face and even overcome the problems.

Instrument Making

An important dimension of music-making is the actual physical instruments used in the musicking. Musicians know that the materials of which their instruments are made, and the way in which their instruments are crafted, can have a substantial impact on their playing and their communication with an audience. In the case of vocal music, the singers' instruments are their own voices, essential parts of their bodies. For instrumentalists, the constructed artefacts that are their instruments become important, although they also use their own bodies to draw music out of these artefacts and to shape the overall sound that they produce. Many musicians believe that the different materials from which their instruments are constructed have a subtle but noticeable impact on the sound produced, and thus the musical feelings of the player and the emotional response of the audience. Dawe (2016) argues that 'materials matter' in the making of musical instruments, both from the viewpoint of the maker, who develops an intimate knowledge of the acoustic and aesthetic properties of the materials, and the player, who is able to sense these qualities in the finished product.

Musical instruments are produced from natural materials, in some cases utilised with only minimal change – such as a didjeridu, a piece of wood hollowed out by termites – and in other cases the result of substantial production effort – such as the shaped metal tube that results in a natural horn. Other instruments are constructed from a large number of diverse parts – such as the wooden frame and soundboard, the metal strings and springs, the bone keys, and the decorative pigments that comprise a keyboard instrument such as a harpsichord.

All such instruments and instrumental components, whether animal, vegetable or mineral in origin, are obtained from a finite resource – the earth on which humanity lives – and so they can all be viewed through the lens of sustainability. Looking at musical instruments in this way, the connections between music-making and the ideas of environmental sustainability may be surprising, as these are areas that are not usually considered together. Some specific examples can be useful to consider, and can suggest some useful starting points for a consideration of the aspects of environmental sustainability that relate to specific instruments.

One familiar example is the use of ivory for the 'natural' keys on a piano, or the 'accidental' keys on a harpsichord. Poaching is a serious problem for elephant populations, and international trade in ivory has been banned or restricted since the 1989 meeting of CITES, the Convention on International Trade in Endangered Species of Wild Flora and Fauna (see http://cites.org). However, smuggling and illegal or 'loophole' sales are still reducing elephant numbers, down to around 400,000 currently. Other animal parts or products have been, or are still being, used in the making of musical instruments. The charango, a small Andean stringed instrument, was traditionally made using the shell of an armadillo as its resonator, but this has been replaced with a wooden shell. Strings for musical instruments used to be made from 'catgut', from the intestines of animals such as sheep and cattle, and gut strings are still favoured in early music instruments such as lutes and viols for their specific properties.

Much more common is the use of rare woods in the making of wind instruments such as recorders and wooden Baroque flutes, and stringed and keyboard instruments. Traditionally, various woods had specific uses in instrument construction. European boxwood is favoured for recorders and flutes, although many other woods, such as rosewood and ebony, or the softer fruit and maple woods can be used. Spruce is commonly used for the soundboards of keyed and stringed instruments, walnut for the decorative backs and sides of guitars and mandolins, ebony and rosewood for fingerboards and pegs, and Pernambuco wood for the bows. Although these materials are not banned, international trade in the rarer and more endangered species of wood is regulated by CITES, and permits are required for import or export.

It may seem that brass instruments, as well as instrument parts made of metal, have fewer problems, but mining itself and the consequent smelting processes have a large environmental footprint. While the amount of metal in a brass instrument is very small compared to the total production of its component metals, usually copper and zinc, there is still an aspect of environmental sustainability to be considered in making and using such an instrument. The situation is more complex in the context of electronic music, where computers and components are constructed and powered by batteries built using rare earth elements such as neodymium, cerium, and lanthanum. Despite their name, these metallic elements are abundant on earth, although they appear in very small concentrations. They are obtained as by-products of other mining operations, separated and purified by multiple complex processes, and hence presenting a variety of problems concerning sustainability, social and economic, as well as environmental (McLellan, Corder, Golev, & Ali, 2014).

From the point of view of environmental sustainability, the basic problem, highlighted by the 'resources' view of sustainability, is the potential overuse of natural resources in the context of increasing numbers of musicians (and increasing population). The 'justice' view may also apply if the resources become inaccessible for particular groups of people, or if the extraction or harvesting of the resources is carried out under inequitable conditions, a situation that seems to occur in mining operations in less developed countries.

In the current era of mass production, a decision to use a particular material in the manufacture of a common musical instrument such as a guitar can have a large effect on the supply of that material. There is no easy solution; even vocal musicians use resources in music-making. Certainly, rare and endangered materials such as ivory and precious woods can be substituted by more common ones like bone and more ordinary woods, or replaced by materials such as plastics, as has occurred in making covers for piano keys. However, plastics – or any other replacement materials – still have an environmental footprint, which may be less than the ivory or metal they replace but will not be negligible. A useful approach is the investigation of alternative materials, such as the use of more common Australian native woods, or even fibreglass, for the construction of stringed instruments. Traditions in which sustainable, easily grown and replaced materials are utilised – such as bamboo for flutes in the UK and *shakuhachi* in Japan is another possibility. An added benefit in these cases is the tradition of players making their own instruments, representing an important and authentic learning opportunity for music students (Matsunobu, 2013). Above all, the important point is for musicians to ensure that they become aware of the aspects of environmental sustainability in their musical lives and to act in accordance with that awareness.

Composition

The natural environment has always been a potent source of inspiration for composers. Think, for example, of Antonio Vivaldi's 1725 violin concerti *The Four Seasons*. In these concerti, one for each season, Vivaldi represented the sounds of the natural world – babbling brooks, a violent storm, frozen landscapes, crackling fires – the animals inhabiting it – twittering birds, buzzing flies, a barking dog – and the humans present – a sleeping goatherd, dancing peasants, a party of hunters. The works were accompanied by four sonnets, thought to have been written by Vivaldi himself, which highlighted the environmental references. These concerti were among the earliest examples of programme music, musical works with a specific narrative element.

A contemporary example of the same approach, from the 2019 Sydney Vivid Festival, is Christine Pan's *Left on Seen*, written for wind quintet and recorder quartet (available at https://soundcloud.com/christinepanmusic performed by Ensemble Terra and The Judgment of Paris). The work utilises theatrical and musical effects, including frequent improvisatory sections, to portray the movements, shadows, and colours of birds of various species flying across the glass-domed ceiling of the Bloedel Conservatory in Vancouver, Canada. The environment, both the specific aviary and the general avian environment, is an essential element of the work.

Environmental sustainability becomes connected with composition in cases where the composer draws inspiration from the environment to highlight some specific or general environmental problem, and uses that as a basis for constructing their composition. In the process, they focus their audience's attention on the dimension of sustainability, increasing their awareness of the problem, challenging their views and attitudes, and sometimes even provoking them to modify their behaviours. This process occurs in a non-rational way that has an effect through emotional rather than logical persuasion. It utilises the ability of music to affect people's ideas and beliefs through such channels. Artists have an essential role in reflecting on society as it is, identifying a range of problems with current ways of being and behaving, and suggesting solutions to such problems. Composers are embedded in their society, and are a reflection of society's attitudes and feelings, but they can also lead society in directions that many people would not naturally take. While many aspects of life and society could be the inspiration for artistic work, there is currently a particular importance and urgency about those that are based on the notion of environmental sustainability.

Kahn (2013) discusses the history of environmental activism in song, predominantly in the US and popular music context, tracing examples back to the 19th century – the earliest seems to be from 1837, a song titled

'Woodman! Spare that Tree!', and maybe the most famous is Joni Mitchell's 1969 'Big Yellow Taxi'. Although the topic of these songs is environmental sustainability, as is the activism that is necessary to promote it, it seems that the most important aspect of the message is the text, carried by the music that ensures its reception and proliferation. A greater focus on the music is shown in two related contemporary reworkings of Vivaldi's *Four Seasons*. In 2019, Hamburg's Elbphilharmie Orchestra presented *For Seasons*, an adaptation of the original using climate change data such as weather extremes and extinction of bird and insect species to modify aspects of the work. 'Deprived of its original musical proportions, the adaptation sees spring and summer become intermixed with harmonic structure decays and instrumental bird voices falling silent' (Bradshaw, 2019). Building on the idea, the Sydney Symphony Orchestra presented *The [Uncertain] Four Seasons* at the 2021 Sydney Festival. Climate prediction data were used to change and distort Vivaldi's creation in a multimedia collaboration between Australian composers, designers, innovators, and scientists. The combination of the Baroque masterpiece and the sounds of a changing world is designed to warn of dangers, offer hope, and inspire action. 'The world pictured here through music is 2040, *if we don't act* – perhaps it is important to recognise that there is still a path back to Vivaldi's *Four Seasons*, if we are willing to take it' (McPherson, 2021).

In a more obvious way, the topic of a composition, and various musical aspects of the work, can raise awareness and initiate thought and debate about environmental sustainability. Many recent compositions make explicit reference to current environmental problems faced in the context of the work. One example is Stuart Greenbaum's choral work *Antarctica* (composed in 2002), scored for treble choir, a pair of violins and organ, which sets a text by Ross Baglin about the rise in sea levels caused by melting polar icecaps. Daniel Blinkhorn's *frostbYte – CO_2* (composed in 2018) is an acoustic and audio-visual commentary on the effect of climate change, in this case set in Svalbard in the Arctic, and scored for saxophone, video, and still images (see https://vimeo.com/263694952). Simon Barker's *Urgency! Drum Chant for Kiribati* was 'played and developed in solidarity with communities and ecosystems facing upheaval due to climate change' (see www.youtube.com/watch?v=dm-XgTUkGk0) and the composer describes the research process behind its composition, based on his extensive experience with barefoot running (Barker, 2021).

The Sydney Chamber Opera (https://sydneychamberopera.com/) programme *Breaking Glass* (performed in 2020) comprises four compositions by participants in the Sydney Conservatorium of Music's *Composing Women Program*. The production was constructed online from recordings and final rehearsal tapes completed just as the Covid-19 pandemic struck.

It includes *The Invisible Bird* by Bree van Reyk, a work that engages with the environmental problem of species extinction as it tells the story of the Night Parrot, a rare Australian bird that was lost and presumed extinct for almost a century. Lei Liang's composition *A Thousand Mountains, A Million Streams* (composed in 2018) was inspired by the paintings of Chinese landscape artist, Huang Binhong, to explore people's relation with nature in the context of widespread environmental destruction, and to convey the importance of preserving these landscapes to sustain their continued existence. This work was the 2020 winner of the Grawemeyer Award for Music Composition, sometimes referred to as the Nobel Prize for music.

Bringing environmental problems to audiences' attention is an important first step in the role of composition in environmental sustainability. For listeners, such musical compositions can raise awareness of known problems or initiate debate about problems that may have 'flown under the radar', inspire them to make connections to places and modify their environmental behaviours, and finally – and most importantly – to begin work on solutions to problems. A very early example is the US environmentalist 'Boll Weevil Song', written by Gates Thomas in 1897, that led indirectly to the diversification of crops in southern US states in response to the ecological dangers of reliance on a cotton monoculture (Kahn, 2013). A current example is the Dreambox Collective, a group of artists with skills in composition, performance, computers, and media, formed by graduates, students, and staff of the Sydney Conservatorium of Music to 'facilitate performances that respond and raise awareness of the climate emergency and social justice' (www.thedreamboxcollective.com/about-us). Their virtual (online) concert *Big Blue* (performed in 2020) of newly composed works had as its central theme the idea of our personal relationship with water. It was preceded by a local clean-up event of ocean debris, and the audience was invited to suggest changed behaviours to decrease the number of plastics entering waterways.

Touring Musicians

Christian IV, King of Denmark in the first half of the 17th century, was a Renaissance monarch with a wide range of talents and interests, including artistic ones. He employed in his court many musicians from abroad, including at different times groups of singers and instrumentalists from various parts of Europe, particularly Italy and the British Isles. A painting from 1623 at Rosenborg Castle in Copenhagen shows four lavishly dressed court musicians, thought to include the harpist, Darby Scott, and the violist, Thomas Simpson, as well as a lutenist and flautist, who together formed an ensemble that specialised in British music. Another chamber group comprised Italian singers and instrumentalists performing madrigals in the Italian style. According to contemporary accounts, musicians played 'hidden music' in a room beneath the King's antechamber, with the sound coming into the room above through concealed channels. A ceiling painting from around 1620 shows musicians, maybe portraits of the actual court musicians of the time, playing from a gallery above, completing the miraculous illusion (Spohr, 2012).

Musicians have always been travellers, both individually and in groups. Music is an art that depends to a large extent on the combined physical presence of the artists and the audience. In earlier times, such as those of King Christian IV, musicians would have travelled by foot, by horse and carriage, or sometimes by ship. But, in the contemporary world, musical travel is undertaken using a much wider range of conveyances, including aeroplanes, by a much larger group of people, orchestras, and bands as well as chamber groups and soloists, and at much greater distances, often across the world. The environmental impact of such travelling is hugely greater than in former times.

Here are some examples, first in the area of classical music. The Sydney Symphony Orchestra toured Europe in 2018, performing twelve concerts in seven countries, to 'highlight the quality of Australia's arts and culture to the world' (www.sydneysymphony.com/docs?sso_2018_impact_report). They have undertaken eight such tours since 2010, visiting Japan, Korea, and China as well as Europe. San Francisco's Kronos Quartet was founded in 1973 by violinist David Harrington, and has spent almost 50 years performing in a wide range of music genres and in many collaborations with contemporary composers. The quartet 'spends five months of each year on tour, appearing in concert halls, clubs and festivals around the world' (https://kronosquartet.org/kronos-quartet/). The situation is similar in other areas of music. From the Beatles' 1964 World Tour, with performances in Europe, Hong Kong, Australia, and New Zealand, to Elton John's Farewell Yellow Brick Road tour (www.eltonjohn.com/stories/farewell-yellow-brick-road), planned to span three years from 2018, touring has always been a large part of popular music. The megastars may have their own tours, but popular music festivals regularly bring together less well-known bands and give them a chance of live touring performance.

Musical groups – orchestras, chamber groups, popular bands – travel for two main reasons: one is to increase their audience and prestige, the other is to increase their financial returns. The situation is somewhat different with educational institutions. For a conservatorium or music school the main point of a tour is pedagogic, with students learning from the experience of preparing and performing a programme in different locations, and interacting with musicians from different cultures. This was the case, for example, for the Sydney Conservatorium of Music's Wind Symphony tour of Spain in 2019, in which a team of 40 students experienced Spanish musical and architectural culture with performances in Madrid, Valencia, and Barcelona. For audiences, there are also obvious benefits of such tours, including the positive experience of listening to live music, in many cases presented by groups they have never heard previously, often bringing a different cultural background to the playing, and sometimes different music entirely, such as the Australian pieces presented in the Wind Symphony tour. In a similar way, the many individual and smaller groups of student musicians who participate in travel programmes experience important learning from the cultural exchange.

Generally, there has been little discussion of the environmental cost of musical touring, although this has been changing recently. In 2010, the London-based group, Julie's Bicycle, published a comprehensive three-part report on the environmental effects of touring companies – bands, orchestras, and theatres. Volume 2, focusing on orchestras, concludes that touring is a fundamental activity supporting their reach and finance. Orchestras have not generally considered the environmental impacts of touring, and they could make significant improvements in terms of the travel, venues and funding involved. Improved touring models could be developed with appropriate tools, guidance, and training. Further, touring can be a great way to raise the issues of climate change with a wider group of people, and to model the behavioural changes that are required to address the problems (Bottrill & Tsiarta, 2010).

In late 2019, the UK band Coldplay made news with their statement that they would not be touring their new album *Everyday Life* until (and unless) they can work out how to present a sustainable live experience that addresses the associated environmental problems such as flying and single-use plastics (https://futurism.com/touring-musicians-brutal-on-environment). Another UK band, Massive Attack, also weighed in on the discussion of the problem (www.theguardian.com/commentisfree/2019/nov/28/tour-world-massive-attack-band-climate) and announced that they were commissioning the Tyndall Centre for Climate Change Research (https://tyndall.ac.uk/about), run by a consortium of UK universities, to map the carbon footprint of typical popular music tours, investigating the three key areas of band travel, audience transport, and venue – each responsible for about one-third of associated greenhouse emissions.

The Covid-19 pandemic highlighted some possible alternative approaches to the problems. Performances that are livestreamed online (or pre-recorded) have much less of the immediacy of a live performance, but there are some benefits for performers (ability to pre-record the playing, sometimes from the comfort of home) and for audiences (ability to see the individual players, and to re-experience the performance). Musical groups that have or are developing an online presence may well keep this as a feature when the pandemic situation improves. The Australian Chamber Orchestra, for instance, founded in 1975, describe themselves as a 'major cultural export, performing over 100 times per year in concert halls around Australia and the world' (www.aco.com.au/the-orchestra/our-story). During the pandemic, tours were cancelled, replaced by a digital programme, *ACO HomeCasts* of livestreamed performances, archival concerts, interviews, and playlists. The problems are more acute for newer groups such as Ensemble Apex, founded in 2016 by a group of young musicians from the Sydney Conservatorium of Music. Their planned 2020 concert series was transformed into digital format with a series of innovative online presentations (www.ensembleapex.com/digital-season) that can be viewed on their YouTube channel.

Of course, such virtual experiences will always miss some of the essential elements of live artistic performances. However, there may be compensations. The opera group at the Sydney Conservatorium of Music replaced a planned live production of *Cendrillon* by Jules Massenet with a recorded, filmed, and mimed version in the second half of 2020 (see https://www.youtube.com/playlist?list=PLSFHNq95NCPmu-v0S7yc2DXoDmRqAr9Dx). The opera students partnered with students from NIDA, the National Institute of Dramatic Art, and all of them were exposed to a wider range of experiences and learnt new skills in the process. The resulting film will be seen by a much larger audience group than could have viewed the live production, resulting in a virtual tour of the production.

Ecomusicology

Many areas of music have some connection or relationship with sustainability in some form, as we have shown in this series of case studies. But one sub-discipline of music has a clear and obvious connection with environmental sustainability; indeed, it is essentially based on the consideration of this connection. Ecomusicology is a recent and developing field focused on the relationship between music and environment. The earliest writings to explicitly use the term are from the 21st century, although its roots go back much further. As an interdisciplinary area of music, it has a growing role in raising awareness of, and developing a theoretical approach to, environmental problems and their relationship with ecology via their connections with sound and music.

Prolific writer and researcher in ecomusicology Jeff Todd Titon (2013) states that ecomusicology 'combines ecocriticism with (ethno)musicology. It is the study of music, culture, sound and nature in a period of environmental crisis' (p. 8), and points out clearly that 'sustainability is one of the main concerns of ecomusicologists' (p. 9). Titon's writings are a good place to begin any investigation of the breadth of ideas and topics encompassed by ecomusicology; some of his earlier and new essays have recently been published in book form (Titon, 2020). He maintains a blog at https://sustainablemusic.blogspot.com/ where one can easily access discussion on a wide variety of subjects. Examples include banning leaf blowers due to their noise pollution (April 22, 2020), the coronavirus soundscape (April 7, 2020), sustaining music by sustaining insects (February 16, 2020), music's carbon footprint (July 3, and September 29, 2019), animal sound communication and human language (August 1, 2019), whale sound and sustainability (May 30, 2019), the sound of wind on Mars (December 27, 2018) and sound baths and sound walks (September, 2018).

Another useful resource is the book *Current Directions in Ecomusicology*, edited by Allen and Dawe (2016). In their introductory chapter (Ecomusicologies), the editors present various responses to the question 'what is ecomusicology?' They begin with straightforward formulations such as 'Environmental studies plus music/sound studies equal ecomusicology', and 'Ecomusicology considers musical and sonic issues, both textual and performative, related to ecology and the natural environment' (both p. 1). They point out that the most important keywords involved in ecomusicology – music and sound, culture and society, nature and environment – are complex and admit a range of interpretations. They formulate a vision for the field as a connection of artistic and scientific enquiry and highlight its essential importance:

> The relevance of ecomusicology comes from its attendant possibilities for adjusting cultural and environmental norms, particularly via teaching. Music and sound can be further media to communicate important ecological ideas and encourage action regarding environmental and sustainability issues.
>
> (p. 4)

The following 19 chapters by various authors present a connected web of ideas and views of ecomusicology. Here are some examples to give a flavour of the whole collection. Boyle and Waterman (2016, Chapter 2) compare and contrast the methodologies used by animal behaviour ecologists studying bird-song and by ethnomusicologists studying performing groups. Both use observation of behaviour; the former are mostly quantitative while the latter are mostly qualitative (and, of course, the human participants are also able to communicate verbally). Simonett (2016, Chapter 7) writes about the musical world-views of the Yoreme indigenous people in Northwestern Mexico. Their ceremonial music and dance acts as a 'sentient ecology', bringing humans into communication with the ecological world and the other creatures therein. The flautist playing bird-song in a trance becomes the bird and engages directly and experientially with the landscape they inhabit. Windsor (2016, Chapter 12) critiques the distinctions between nature and culture, and their reflection in noise and music, as well as 'everyday' and 'musical' listening. He concludes that education in music, particularly higher education, is in need of more direct engagement with the sonic dimensions of events, objects, and spaces (including, but not limited to, 'free' improvisation). Editor Allen (2016) returns in Chapter 20 to investigate the writings in a mid-19th-century Italian journal of music, drama, and literature of a 'nascent ecomusicological community' on the intersections between music, culture, and nature. Examples focus on birds trained to sing operatic extracts, forest soundscapes as inspiration for human music, and singing mice and apes. The other chapters continue a fascinating investigation of the varied connections between the aural and the environmental world.

In terms of conception, writings in ecomusicology, such as the examples presented earlier, are predominantly based on the 'justice' conception of sustainability in an 'integrated' setting. They commonly position music as a tool towards achieving environmental and ecological sustainability, essentially presenting a view of 'music *for* sustainability'. In a little over a decade (although with roots going back much further), the emerging field of ecomusicology has been the subject of conferences and special issues of journals, and has brought attention to the relevance of music to the contemporary environmental crisis and the possible contributions that it can offer to a solution.

Perhaps the most important of these is the ability to bring ecological problems to a wider audience. Ryan writes (in Allen & Dawe, 2016, p. 64) that players of eucalypt instruments are 'uniquely positioned to sensitize audiences to respect and rethink valuable environments as they imitate and explain the natural sounds of the bush'. Education at all levels provides what is likely to be the largest and broadest possible audience. A book by Shevock (2018) offers a comprehensive investigation of 'eco-literate music pedagogy' based on his experiences teaching university classes and summer music camps, as well as his background as a philosopher and researcher. He identifies the importance of viewing music as an activity undertaken by all living things, linking music and nature based on connection to local places extending to global ecological crises. He includes many practical examples of eco-literate musical behaviour that would be a useful resource for music teachers at any level.

5 Economic Sustainability in Music

Introduction

In its broadest terms, the economic sustainability of music is concerned with musical practices that support long-term economic activity without negatively impacting social, environmental, and cultural aspects of the community. The earlier definition of economic sustainability mentioned in Chapter 2 (www.thwink.org/sustain/glossary/EconomicSustainability.htm) as 'the ability of an economy to support a defined level of economic production indefinitely' can be applied directly to the musical (or cultural) aspects of the economy. The common measure in terms of gross domestic product (GDP) is not very useful here, particularly with the standard economic goal of continual increase (flat GDP is referred to as 'stagnation' and, even worse, falling GDP as 'recession'). A better economic goal could be to optimise the long-term economic quality of life for those living and their descendants, maybe by reducing the proportion of people living below a minimum economic standard. It is an appropriate challenge to consider how music could contribute to this.

The case studies in this chapter investigate intersections between music and the economic pillar of sustainability, the second of the classic three pillars. For musicians, the economic aspect may not be the most obvious aspect of sustainability to consider, but as these case studies show, there are many aspects of musical life and the business of music that have an economic dimension. The first case study looks at the economic cost of music from the point of view of the consumer, through a historical survey of the most common formats in which music has been made available to listeners, from the wax cylinders of the late 19th century, through various disc and tape formats, to the contemporary digital downloads and streaming. There are various costs – financial, material, and other – for each of the formats, including the digital format. The second case study investigates the contribution of the music industry to the economic life of the nation. Various

DOI: 10.4324/9781003044642-5

national reports indicate that cultural industries, including music, make a larger contribution to economic well-being than is generally acknowledged, and in particular, investment in musical entrepreneurship pays valuable dividends for the city, region, or country that makes it.

Many practising musicians are essentially small business owners, juggling the demands of advertising, contracting, supplying related services such as teaching, and keeping business records, as well as actually creating or playing music. The third case study explores the aspects of economic sustainability involved in the construction and running of musical careers, particularly the very common 'portfolio' careers that combine a number of dimensions of musical work. The final case study addresses a specific problem in musical working life, the limitation of musical opportunity for early-career musicians caused by the tendency of older musicians to continue in their positions well past traditional retirement age. The discussion is set in the context of academic work in conservatories and universities, but could apply to other circumstances such as orchestral work.

In the context of economic sustainability, the 'resources' view of sustainability is the obvious one – in this case, the economic view of distribution of and access to resources, and the associated costs, financial but also social and environmental. However, it is a small step to the 'justice' view, considering the common inequity of access to resources, and the various possibilities for ethical action to address these inequalities. The case studies in this chapter are all based on the 'resources' view of sustainability, and at several points show a clear inclusion of the 'justice' view.

The Cost of Music

Although music and economics seem to be quite different areas of human endeavour, there is an increasing amount of attention paid to their intersection, the economics of music, and the more general field of the economics of arts and culture. Whenever music is viewed as a commodity or service, brought into being by producers and made available to consumers, then economic investigation of allocation of resources, production of goods, distribution, and consumption is indicated. Despite first impressions, every form of music-making and consuming has an economic aspect, and hence a cost in terms of economic sustainability. Such a cost is not limited only to the economic aspect, but is also felt in other dimensions – environmental, social, and cultural – even though this case study focuses on the economic aspects.

A study by Brennan and Devine (2020) investigated the cost of music, both in economic and in environmental (and other) terms. The investigation was deliberately framed in terms of cost rather than value, as a contrast to the more usual discussion of aspects of culture in terms of their value. The authors focused on the aspect of sound recordings, and asked the related questions: what is the most sustainable way for musicians to distribute their recordings, and what is the most sustainable way for consumers to listen to them? Answers to such questions are increasingly important to musicians deciding whether to produce physical copies of their recordings, and if so, in what format, in addition to making them available on digital music platforms for purchase and download by their audience. And musicians are increasingly considering other aspects of sustainability, as well as the economic aspects.

Brennan and Devine begin with a historical economic perspective, investigating how the price of recordings has changed from the late 19th century to the early 21st century. During this time, seven economically significant technologies have been utilised, namely wax or celluloid cylinder and phonograph, 78 rpm shellac disc and gramophone, vinyl LP album and turntable, cassette tape and cassette player, compact disc and CD player, digital album download and digital audio player, streaming platform and streaming device. Specifically, they calculated the approximate cost to consumers for listening to their choice of music at the time when each of these formats was at its peak. As with any economic investigation of this type, various assumptions and decisions have to be made about what data to collect and how to measure them appropriately.

The researchers decided to use the US as the location of the case study, due to availability of the required data. They gathered information on the units produced and/or sold in each year to find the peak year of production for each format. They then obtained information on the contemporary cost of each unit, from sales data or advertisements, adjusted for inflation to 2018 US dollar (US$) prices. Finally, they obtained data on average salaries for US citizens, given as median weekly pre-tax earnings of full-time wage and salary earners, and again adjusted them for inflation. Post-tax earnings might have been more realistic to use, but that would have required even more assumptions. Although the questions can be expressed simply, the economic and statistical work to obtain answers is rather complex!

The summary results of this quantitative investigation are shown in Table 5.1. Several points can be made. The cost in US$ increased dramatically with the introduction of the LP, but it has been coming down since then, and in 2021, is lower than it has ever been. The cost in percentage of weekly salary has been decreasing, with only a slight rise with the LP, and in 2021, it is also at its lowest ever. The units produced and sold have been rising steadily, although it is difficult to make an appropriate comparison with the latest digital formats.

52 Economic Sustainability in Music

Table 5.1 The cost of music

Technology	Peak Year	Cost US$	% Weekly Salary	Units (million)
Phonograph cylinder	1907	$13.88	(7.4% *)	28
78 rpm disc	1947	$10.89	3.8%	325
Vinyl LP album	1977	$28.55	4.8%	344
Cassette tape	1988	$16.66	2.4%	450
CD	2000	$21.59	2.6%	943
Digital album	2013	$11.11	1.2%	118 (1340 **)
Streaming	(2020)	($9.99/month)	(1.0%)	(76 ***)

* estimated from data in surrounding years
** including 1/20 of single-track downloads
*** latest estimate 76 million users or 23% 'user penetration'

The availability of digital access to music has resulted in a fundamental change to the economic model from a commodity industry, where people buy physical copies of music to keep, to a service industry, where people pay for access to digital music stored in a remote location. The costs for a digital album could be comparable with costs for previous formats, although the units are less comparable (the figure in brackets includes downloads of 'singles', assuming that 20 of them are equivalent to an album). The costs for streaming are not comparable with earlier costs, as they represent a monthly outlay giving access to essentially unlimited amounts of music. Nor are the units comparable, as they represent millions of people with subscriptions, and each user will be listening to many hours of music each month.

At this stage, the economic investigation broadens. The cost of music includes a range of other costs that are harder to quantify, not paid for directly by the consumer, and are most often completely out of sight or mind. Brennan and Devine discuss the environmental costs by looking at the materials used to make recordings, where they come from and how they are disposed of at the end of their life. They also discuss the social costs in terms of the – usually very poor – labour conditions of the people involved in the production processes. It may seem at first sight that these costs do not apply to the most recent digital formats, but that is emphatically not the case.

Physical materials and energy generation are needed to support the whole infrastructure involved in digital storage and access to music, and social conditions of people involved in production of the required devices are often as bad as for any earlier group of producers. Indeed, the authors show that, from an environmental viewpoint, the equivalent greenhouse gas (GHG) cost of digital formats is higher than it has ever been for previous technologies. They estimate that the annual cost is somewhere between 200 (optimistic) and 350 (pessimistic) million kg GHG per year, compared with around 150 in the LP, cassette, and CD era. Even calculated per person to allow for increasing population, the optimistic estimate is at around the same level as previously, while the pessimistic estimate is almost twice as high. Of course, from an environmental perspective, it is total cost that is important. Much more detail is given in the article (Brennan & Devine, 2020), and an extended discussion in Devine's (2019) book.

Economic Contribution of Music

It is generally accepted that industries such as manufacturing and construction, and activities such as agriculture and retailing, contribute to the economic life of a country. Manufacturing and construction produce new machines and buildings, agriculture produces the food that we need while retailing keeps the economic wheels turning as goods are sold from wholesaler to retailer to consumer. While it is less obvious, a field such as music also makes a contribution to economic life, although it is more problematic to determine the extent of this contribution,

Throsby (2008) investigates a number of models for the economic role of music. In all of them, music is classified as a core cultural industry, maybe within a broader framework of creative industries, although the combined term 'cultural and creative industries' (or CCI) is also used. As Throsby points out, the terms 'cultural' and 'creative' admit a wide variety of interpretations, leading to different assessments of their economic role. In general, however, cultural activity generally requires creative input and produces something that has symbolic value beyond the commercial and utilitarian, thus positioning cultural industries as a subset of creative industries.

The UIS (UNESCO Institute of Statistics, 2009), for instance, defines culture as 'the set of distinctive spiritual, material, intellectual and emotional features of society or a social group, that encompasses not only art and literature, but lifestyles, ways of living together, value systems, traditions and beliefs' (p. 9). The UIS model specifies a number of cultural domains, including 'Performance and Celebration' in which music in its entirety is located (p. 24). The report states clearly that:

> The cultural sector in some developed countries is more economically important (at least in employment terms) than a number of older established industries (e.g. mining and car manufacturing) and it contributes

significantly to national export earnings. While the economic impact of the cultural sector in the developing world is, at present, less evident with regard to employment, export earnings may be significant.

(p. 12)

Supporting this assessment, Throsby (2008, p. 225) writes that studies of the cultural industries 'demonstrate that the arts are not some minor economic backwater but account for a larger proportion of GDP or of aggregate employment than the casual observer might have imagined'. Focusing specifically on music rather than the cultural industries as a whole, it seems that the contribution of music to the economic life of Australia (and other countries) is much more than generally acknowledged. Music here comprises a full range of activities, described in the UIS report (2009, p. 19) as a cycle of five stages: creation, production, dissemination, exhibition or transmission, and consumption or participation, as well as the associated activities of archiving or preserving, and education or training. The economic contribution is sometimes analysed using the notion of the 'cultural production chain', exemplified by the path from musical idea to song, to published print, to live performance, to recording and internet streaming. At other times, the assessment of economic contribution is made on the basis of statistics collected on aspects of cultural activity; Throsby (2020) gives more details of 'cultural statistics', identifying many of the difficulties involved in quantifying the economic aspects of cultural behaviour.

Individual musicians and music organisations, both small and large, make a significant financial contribution to any nation. In the Australian context, a landmark report carried out by the University of Tasmania for the Live Music Office (2014) concluded that for every dollar (A$) invested by the community in live music over A$3 is returned. The report is a carefully argued assessment using standard economic models and justifiable economic methods. The benefits of live music-making were measured as A$15.7 billion in three main areas – commercial, civic, and individual – and further benefits such as volunteering, and avoidance of costs associated with health and criminal systems were identified but not quantified. The costs of live music, both direct and opportunity costs, were estimated at A$5 billion, giving a benefit-to-cost ratio of over three-to-one. The report gives detailed justification of these steps and makes for interesting reading, particularly for those who have some quantitative or economic background.

Another report, by Music Australia (2016) focused on contemporary music. The *National Contemporary Music Plan* estimated that this music sector contributes A$4–A$6 billion to the Australian economy, more than manufacturing or health care, with recorded music-making a particularly significant contribution. The plan states that contemporary music generates about 65,000 jobs, contributes strongly to Australia's export earnings, and is a key component of national growth. It points out that many Australians, some 12% of the population, regularly attend live music, with a total of around 40 million visits annually. Although it focuses on the economic aspects, the plan identifies the important role of music in the cultural life of the country, and its contribution to the population's health, well-being and social capital. Not surprisingly, the report calls for more investment, particularly in the form of tax incentives, but also private and public partnerships, to support the continued growth of the sector, both domestically, and internationally.

Throsby (2008) writes about the cultural industries as a whole that 'the arts can be seen as part of a wider and more dynamic sphere of economic activity, with links through to the information and knowledge economies, fostering creativity, embracing new technologies and feeding innovation' (p. 229). In particular, he identifies their role in economically rejuvenating depressed urban or regional areas by stimulating growth in heritage, performing arts, museums, and galleries as attractions for increased tourism, and as a basis for high-tech industries such as video game production and website design. Such suggestions point out the balance needed between the instrumental role of culture in economic production and its essential cultural purpose.

In the final analysis, many artists, including musicians, are not motivated only or even primarily by money. Throsby (2008, p. 227) points out the economist's view that 'creative workers care passionately about the quality of their product and will therefore often behave in ways that are contrary to the predictions of rational labour market theory'! Although investigating the contribution of music from an economic viewpoint is an interesting approach, and the statistical information obtained is valuable, in the final analysis economic theory and cultural statistics are not adequate to explain every aspect of human life, particularly cultural life.

Music Careers as Small Businesses

In previous times, a career path could lead from musical studies or apprenticeship to a job as a player in an orchestra, ensemble or company – or some other similar job that is continuing and stable – and then to a lifelong career as a musician. Such traditional career paths are increasingly less likely in the early 21st century, and in particular, they are definitely rare in music. More commonly, musicians will move from their studies to a number of separate casual or occasional jobs or gigs, accessed through professional networks. These jobs may be augmented by some more regular work as a teacher, and possibly supported by more stable employment, for instance as a part-time manager of a musical group, or even in some job completely unrelated to music.

Such a career path is sometimes known as a 'portfolio' career – the term implying a gathering of various job opportunities – one-off, casual, part-time – into a grouping that can provide a living taken together, and can be 'rebalanced' at various times depending on the available work options. Some writers refer to the more extreme portfolio careers as 'protean', named after the mythical sea-god Proteus, son of Poseidon and brother of Triton, who had the ability to foresee the future but would change form to avoid having to do so (Hannan, 2012, gives an intriguing and personal description of such a career). At best, a portfolio career is assembled from professional opportunities through professional networks and supports the individual musician's growth of skills and experiences. At worst, the protean career constantly changes musical shape and is designed to avoid the future dangers of narrowing opportunities, closing of musical companies, drying up of teaching opportunities, and other such problems that can arise.

A commonly used classification of creative employment activities – musical or otherwise – is referred to as the 'Creative Trident'; it is simply (three-quarters of) a two-way classification of employment as creative or not in an industry that is creative or not. Creative workers in creative industries are referred to as 'specialist', such as a bass guitarist in a jazz ensemble or a singer in an opera company. Non-creative workers in creative industries are classed as 'support', for example, the administrator of a chamber orchestra or the financial manager of a rock band. Creative workers in non-creative industries are called 'embedded'; examples are a music therapist working in an aged-care home and a composer writing or selecting music for a retail chain. The missing quarter, relating to non-creative work in non-creative industries, is held to be outside the Trident. The model has several flaws, most obviously in its explicit identification of creative versus non-creative. Many 'non-creative' industries such as manufacturing or health care have obvious creative aspects. In particular, teaching (of music, or anything else) is positioned in the model as non-creative work – an assessment that would be challenged by the majority of musicians with teaching experience.

Surveys and other sources of data show that most musicians do not identify themselves in only one of the Trident classifications, but rather in multiple groups, including very often the last, the non-creative work in non-creative industries. One particular aspect of musical work that is a constant for many musicians is their teaching role, sometimes in schools or conservatoires, most often privately, but there are many others who include as part of their portfolio work in some situation completely unrelated to their musical life, maybe a job as a retail assistant or manager of a café. Bennett and colleagues' (2014) survey of creative workers in Perth, including a range of artists considerably broader than just those in a musical area, showed that fewer than one in six of the respondents were aligned with a single Trident classification, while the majority partook of multiple classifications, including the missing quarter of the Trident, non-creative work in a non-creative industry.

An immediate consequence of the widespread nature of portfolio careers in the music world is that many musicians are essentially in charge of running their own micro business, and most professional musical activity includes a business element as a small or sometimes substantial component. This comprises many and varied activities. For a small ensemble such as a jazz group or a chamber choir, the first aspect would be securing funds for running the ensemble, through writing grant applications or by seeking philanthropic contributions, maybe through crowd funding. Then there is the aspect of promotion, which may involve constructing and maintaining a website, advertising in relevant places, and keeping records of previous employers and audience members. The financial aspects include finding and hiring venues, deciding on ticket prices, payment for musicians, and pricing for hiring the ensemble. Making recordings introduces another layer of financial negotiation, including promotion and sale of the product, physical or online. Larger ensembles such as an orchestra or an opera company may have staff who handle the business aspects. Individual musicians will need to engage with many of the previous aspects, and they may also need to schedule and manage teaching activities.

Many music schools and conservatoriums include courses that identify and develop the business skills required for a successful career as a musician. At the Sydney Conservatorium of Music, for instance, the Jazz Business Skills option – jazz players have always formed groups and run small businesses – became a Business Skills course, available for any interested student, and is part of a compulsory 'capstone' project in which students form groups and develop business plans for their continuation. Orchestras such as Ensemble Apex (www.ensembleapex.com/) and smaller ensembles such as the Dreambox Collective (www.thedreamboxcollective.com/) show that new graduates with appropriate business skills can create and run successful musical groups.

Intergenerational Equity of Music Careers

A basic principle of economic sustainability is that economic capital, including the possibility of meaningful employment, is passed from one generation to the next without any substantial decrease. As one generation ages and moves towards retirement, the next generation is being trained to take their place and their jobs. Such replacement has an ethical dimension, independent of any assumption of negative stereotypes of ageing. In the context of music, there are some musicians who undertake higher research degrees in order to move into academia to teach the next generation in universities and conservatoriums (orchestras could be another example). In some cases, incumbent academics stay in their positions for a long time past any usual retirement age, and it has been suggested that this may be restricting the careers of younger musicians. Although academic employment is attractive to only a minority of musicians – those with the skills and desire to continue researching and teaching at the highest level – the possible 'blocking' of their career paths is a problem of intergenerational equity.

Some countries specify a general retirement age, which applies to anyone working as an academic; such is the case, for instance, in Singapore, Japan, and most European countries. Other countries have removed any compulsory retirement age, usually to avoid any form of age discrimination; the US and Australia are examples. Sometimes the problem is presented as a difficulty in finding younger workers to replace an ageing workforce, other times the problem is identified as younger workers – academics or other professionals – being 'blocked' from career progression by older workers occupying senior positions. Many articles and reports in the popular press show various views of the problem, although they tend to talk about the labour force as a whole. Governments and economists usually point out that the extra money put into the system by older workers increases overall economic activity and hence the jobs available for younger workers. This may be less true in the academic context than in the general workforce, and seems to be particularly problematic in music. Older musician academics often find themselves in very comfortable positions and are reluctant to move into retirement; younger musicians, would-be academics, are unable to find appropriate positions.

Almost two decades ago, Hugo (2005) researched the problem in Australian academia. He discussed the demographics of the large numbers of 'baby boomers' passing through the academic workforce, causing a noticeable 'age heaping'. He pointed out that Australian academia contained an even larger proportion of older people than the general workforce. He concluded that there would soon be problems replacing academic positions, let alone catering for the growth in participation of university students, occurring at that time and projected to continue. In the previous period of such imbalance, in the late 1970s and early 1980s, many positions were filled by international recruitment, a solution that would not work again due to overseas competition. He stated that 'Australian universities are facing their greatest recruiting task for three decades' (p. 341). Hugo's work was carried out in academia generally, with some examples from specific disciplines, but music was not identified as having any problem. He concluded with various recommendations, including mentoring of promising talented students and development of family-friendly policies to support the participation of more women. He predicted a boom situation for younger would-be academics wanting to start careers over the following decade or more. Sadly, this has not eventuated.

The UK government removed the national default retirement age in 2011, and Blackham (2015) investigated the effects compared with the situation in Australia, where the mandatory retirement age had been removed progressively from the 1990s. In the UK, a workplace was able to keep a fixed retirement age as long as legitimate justification was provided. This was done by the two most famous UK universities, Oxford and Cambridge, and the latter's webpage shows explicit reasons for this: 'The University operates a retirement age for University officers in order to: ensure intergenerational fairness and career progression; enable effective succession planning...' (University of Cambridge, 2019).

Blackham's analysis was undertaken in academia in general, with a particular focus on law. Once again, there was no mention of music, although she presented different views from six case studies of Australian universities. There was general agreement that 'academics are a very, very different breed of individuals' compared to ordinary employees as most of them believe that 'academia is more than a job... [it's] a way of life' (p. 518) and so they don't want to stop working or retire. As the majority of academics are in more senior positions, the financial cost of their salaries limits their universities' ability to employ younger academics. While the demographics were very much on the side of needing younger replacements, various factors worked against this.

One of the key factors was the growing casualisation of the academic workforce (Blackham, 2020), a phenomenon that has increased to the point where the majority of academic teaching is carried out by staff on casual and short fixed-term contracts. While the proportion of senior academics increases, the deficit in academic work is being taken up by casual and short fixed-term contract staff rather than career academics. Most young academic staff are on precarious hourly or short-term contracts focusing on teaching rather than research, in poor conditions, and without any defined career path. Indeed, such work becomes career limiting if extended over more than a couple of years.

Much of the previous discussion has been in the context of higher education generally. In an informal discussion with music heads from conservatoriums around the Pacific, many countries that had no compulsory retirement age reported problems with academics 'hanging on', and financial problems of paying salaries of senior staff as well as equity problems of finding positions for the next generation of musicians. Voluntary redundancies for older staff – implemented in Australian universities during the Covid-19 pandemic – represent a possible solution. One of Blackham's interviewees stated that at their university, some of their older academics were encouraged to retire onto the 'pension payroll', making room for a younger academic, in exchange for an honorary appointment, and such an appeal to altruism was often successful! One respondent at another university felt it was 'incumbent on all of us to question whether we have reached our use-by-date' (p. 528), explicitly making intergenerational fairness a personal responsibility.

6 Social Sustainability in Music

Introduction

The four case studies in this chapter focus on the intersections between music and sustainability in the area of social sustainability, the final pillar of the classic 'three-pillar model'. Social sustainability is concerned with establishing and maintaining the conditions in society that support human well-being in all its forms, from the well-being of individuals to the well-being of humanity as a whole, and everything in between. This could include, for instance, the role of music in promoting inclusion, bridging isolation, developing cross-cultural understandings, and valuing diversity and tolerance. The examples given in this chapter demonstrate some ideas for the ways in which music can be used to achieve these aims, and they can suggest further possibilities.

The first case study looks at the role of musical institutions, specifically symphony orchestras, in increasing social sustainability. A symphony orchestra has an obvious social role, to play a culturally important style of music for people and to introduce them to a repertoire of great classical works and maybe others less well known. However, as a social institution, it also has a role to contribute to the social health of the community in which it finds itself, and some examples of exactly how this can be done are described. The second case study changes perspective from the professional musicians to those members of the community who are interested in participating in musicking. Research and experience concur in finding a wide range of benefits resulting from participating in music, maybe playing or singing in a community ensemble or choir, or attending musical events where some form of participation is encouraged; anything from a bamboo pipe workshop to a sing-along at the local pub.

The third case study investigates the relationship between music and health, formalised in the sub-discipline of music known as music therapy. Music therapy is the professional use of music as a medical or psychological

DOI: 10.4324/9781003044642-6

intervention to improve people's physical and mental quality of life. It seems to be effective in a wide variety of life stages and contexts, from pre-term babies through to aged-care homes, from specific illnesses such as cancers to more general conditions such as anxiety. There are many times when social conditions are far from ideal, and supporting human well-being requires challenging these conditions, and working to improve society. The final case study looks at the powerful role that music can have in achieving these aims. Tyrannical rulers, corporations, and societies have always feared musicians – and artists in general – for their ability to challenge unjust behaviour and lead the transformation to a more equitable society.

In these four case studies, the 'resources' view of sustainability is certainly in evidence, in this case, focusing on the social resources of community and society. However, social sustainability is underpinned by notions of social equity, justice, and values, so the 'justice' view is also often in evidence. Since inequality and injustice are frequently entrenched within society, there is always the question of whether social sustainability is best achieved with significant societal change, or whether local, piecemeal approaches are more appropriate. Perhaps there is a role for both approaches – incremental local change as well as occasional radical system change.

Symphony Orchestras and Sustainability

The standard or typical symphony orchestra, with groups of strings, woodwinds, brass, and percussion, augmented if necessary, by other instruments such as piano or harp, or even voices, was established in the late 18th century and consolidated in the early 19th century. It was a product of its time, and most particularly of the growing middle class who had leisure and money to attend its concerts. The orchestra's form was developed in response to the writing of Beethoven, then expanded to accommodate the music of, first Wagner, and then Mahler. Although able to accommodate extensive variations, the symphony orchestra is a particularly Western 19th-century combination of musical forces. In what ways, then, might the symphony orchestra play a role in sustainability, and in particular, the social aspects of sustainability, in the global context of the early 21st century?

One feature of the symphony orchestra that seems to be mentioned often and in a variety of contexts is its use as a metaphor for society. The function of the various parts of the orchestra, the relationships between them, and the overall aims of the music-making can be seen as a reflection in miniature of the social world in which the orchestra is situated. The metaphor can focus on the various ways in which power is distributed, the economic and managerial aspects of the work, the social roles of its various components, and the balance between individual actions and collective goals. The metaphor is often invoked in the business context, possibly due to an idealised conception of the (commercial) benefits obtained from consistent individual behaviour directed towards an organisational goal. More relevant here, Ramnarine (2011) gives an extended discussion of aspects of the metaphor in a musical and sociological context. Her exposition indicates how the idea of a symphony orchestra can play an abstract role in the notion of social sustainability.

A particular aspect of the orchestra as metaphor for society is the position of the leader. An orchestra is generally directed by a conductor, who plays a variety of roles but essentially aims to make the orchestral performance more than the sum of its parts. There are different conceptions of the ways in which a conductor acts as a leader corresponding to different views of leadership in society generally. Is the authority of a conductor rational, due to some established and agreed ways of behaving such as laws, or traditional, due to historic belief in legitimacy of the position, or charismatic, due to particular features of the conductor's personality? And is the conductor's leadership due to authority, or to the stronger idea of power, or maybe the more diffuse idea of influence? Such sociological questions are important for the possible ways in which civil societies can be organised, and their discussion in the microcosmic context of a symphony orchestra can provide useful lessons for society as a whole.

Although a conductor is a feature of symphony orchestras, there are cases where they present their programmes without one. The New York-based Orpheus Chamber Orchestra has, since 1972, worked with a leadership structure in which the musicians interpret the score and make decisions collaboratively. A group such as the Australian Chamber Orchestra often presents works and whole programmes with their Artistic Director, Richard Tognetti, leading from the violin. This leadership model seems to work well with smaller orchestras, and was the most common approach for orchestras in earlier times, such as Baroque orchestras. Indeed, moving beyond the Western classical musical tradition, there are many musical groups in other cultures that have traditions of performance that do not include a conductor. The Balinese gamelan orchestra is one such example. Tempo, rhythm, and transitions between sections are usually indicated by one of the instruments, the *kedang* hand-played drum. Such ensembles increase the range of models of musician interaction, and by extension, of larger social groups.

However, there are further ways in which a symphony orchestra can contribute to aspects of social sustainability in its community, beyond the metaphoric mode. As civic entities, orchestras are in a culturally privileged position to carry out their prime function of presenting to their audiences music that is often Western classical music from the 19th century. Orchestral musicians often come from a comfortable background that has supported their extensive conservatorium training. This background can be utilised to develop greater social responsibility and awareness of the broader and less privileged position of the members of their community. The meaning of the symphony orchestra can be broadened to include musicians and music from other cultures. Repertoire choice can be broadened to include other genres and styles of music, some of it focused on local or wider social problems. The location of performances can be extended beyond the concert hall to venues that could be seen as less exclusive. And community members can be included in planning for, and even performing with, the orchestra.

In this way, a symphony orchestra can provide a model of civic collaboration that can raise awareness of problems of social sustainability and suggest solutions to such problems. In his thesis, Dalton (2018) gives some case studies of US orchestras and lists several strategies for orchestras wishing to become active participants in the life of their communities. These include identifying the cultural distinctness of their community, planning to authentically include this localness, empowering local voices through representation, and even the suggestion to learn from the behaviour of successful sporting teams. Ramnarine (2011) discusses several 'ethnographic' case study examples from the UK. She summarises:

> In various examples of interaction and creative intervention in which inclusion, disadvantage, participation, poverty, peace and green politics are contemplated, symphony orchestras move away from serving only as metaphors of society to being socially-aware participants in orchestrations of civil society.
>
> (p. 348)

Examples can also be drawn from the authors' own local experience. The Sydney Conservatorium of Music's orchestras have regularly been involved in regional tours that include musical collaborations with regional conservatoriums and performances at civic events in local venues. The Sydney Chamber Opera (www.sydneychamberopera.com) presents regular programmes of commissioned works by younger composers designed to engage with social problems, such as the 2020 programme *Breaking Glass* that includes works highlighting depressive disorders (*Her Dark Marauder*, by Georgia Scott) and social problems of transport (*Commute* by Peggy Polias). Such programming contributes towards increasing the relevance of the chamber musical group for a younger audience of the early 21st century.

Participatory Music

There are many research reports that support what musicians know from their own experience, that participating in musical activities brings a whole range of benefits. These include personal benefits such as improved physical and mental health, feelings of pride and accomplishment, and the pleasure and enjoyment that accompany much music-making. They also include social benefits such as creating and maintaining social interactions, developing and strengthening community ties, inclusion of participants from diverse backgrounds, and identifying and working to solve social problems. A review of studies by Lehmberg and Fung (2010) gives more details of the benefits of music participation for healthy senior citizens. The authors point out that such research holds strong potential value for all age groups. In this section we look at the range of ways in which participation in music can contribute towards social sustainability.

Of course, there are many ways to participate in music, including actually playing a musical instrument or singing, listening to a live music performance, or even humming or tapping along with recorded music. An interesting article in this context is the work by Turino (2009). He identifies four distinct fields of music-making and relates them to aspects of sustainable living. Turino does not claim that these four fields cover all possibilities, nor that they are always completely distinct, but they do provide a useful way of thinking about music-making in various contexts, societies, and cultural groups. Each field corresponds to a particular view of sustainability generally, and social sustainability in particular.

'Presentational performance' is maybe the most familiar field of music-making, and is often the first approach that comes to mind when thinking about musical performance. Here a group of musicians – the performers – (or an individual musician) prepare and offer a musical programme to an audience; they present a concert. The performers are expected to be competent at the appropriate level, in some contexts even to the level of virtuosity, to have rehearsed their music, and to make an interesting and entertaining presentation to their audience.

'High-fidelity recording' refers to any process of taking a live performance and turning it into a representation that can be accessed by listeners at another time. Such recordings can be made at a live event or, more commonly, in a studio, sometimes with each musician recording their contribution separately. This process adds extra artistic roles for recording, producing, and engineering the sound. Musicians are well aware that the results can be quite different to a live performance. For much of the world, this field of music is the most common experience, given the widespread availability of vast amounts of music through digital channels.

Beyond the high-fidelity recording, 'studio audio art' involves the creation or manipulation of sounds using electronic instruments or digital techniques to produce a work of art in the form of an electronic recording. Such a work is sometimes referred to as a 'sound sculpture', and in some instances, listeners might even debate whether it is a piece of 'music' at all. A work of studio audio art is not intended to represent or be related to a live performance at all, and is crafted by its composer as a complete and coherent piece.

Broader than a presentational performance, the field of 'participatory performance' refers to contexts where people actively contribute to the overall sound and rhythm of musical activity by clapping, dancing, singing, or playing instruments as an integral part of the activity. In participatory performance there is essentially no distinction between 'artist' and 'audience', and everyone is encouraged, sometimes subtly and sometimes more directly, to participate in some way in the musical activity. The participatory performance is set up in such a way that people with different abilities can contribute in different ways, and the success or otherwise of the event is judged by the amount and quality of the participation. In distinction to the other three fields, participatory music is focused on the social interactions and benefits rather than the finished artistic product. The camp-fire sing- or play-along, the Australian bush dance, and the Christmastime 'carols by candlelight' are examples of participatory song and dance from the Western tradition; Turino gives examples from other cultures, such as the Shona village ceremonies in Zimbabwe.

One particular type of participatory music that features often in discussions and research reports is the community choir. Although many community choirs use a public performance as part of their activities, it is only an occasional step into presentational performance, maybe as a way of legitimising the regular musical activities, as a motivational goal for the choir members, and as a way of extending the social group to include family members and friends – the most common audience at such events. Choirs in various contexts report a similar range of personal and social benefits. As one example among many, Batt-Rawden and Andersen (2020) found that Norwegian women who sang in a choir reported that their singing helped to construct social connections and break down social barriers, and encouraged their sense of connection and belonging. On the basis of interviews with choristers, the authors concluded that choral singing promoted emotional, cognitive, and social health, and was an effective vehicle for tackling social exclusion. Although the term was not specifically mentioned, it is apparent that the choirs were contributing to aspects of social sustainability.

As an alternative expression for participatory music, the term 'community music' is occasionally used. However, in some contexts it implies an interventionist idea, when a particular social problem is identified, and then participatory musical activities are organised to address the problem and to try to enact a solution. A recent example is the community singing from balconies of groups of people under lockdown during the Covid-19 pandemic period in 2020, particularly in Italy and the UK. Such singing had a dramatic effect on group cohesion and morale during a difficult time when most opportunities for social interaction were not available. Another example is the creation of community orchestras such as the Venezuelan El Sistema and the Australian Symphony for Life, designed to spread the benefits of musical engagement to children who would not otherwise have the opportunity.

Music and Health

Many people have been touched by music's emotional power to remember people, places, or events, and to evoke particular moods. This extends to positive responses to music by people with a range of health problems – physical illnesses, dementia, stress and anxiety, substance abuse, developmental and mental problems. The reactions of such people to music in some form can often seem astounding, even miraculous. Music therapy is a method of using music with therapeutic aims by qualified practitioners working with individuals and groups in a range of contexts. Musicking in all its forms is seen as a fundamental human right, able to bring joy, enlightenment, comfort, solace, and growth. Music therapists uphold this right in their professional dealings.

The World Federation of Music Therapy defines the field as an art and science in the following way:

> Music therapy is the professional use of music and its elements as an intervention in medical, educational, and everyday environments with individuals, groups, families, or communities who seek to optimize their quality of life and improve their physical, social, communicative, emotional, intellectual, and spiritual health and wellbeing. Research, practice, education, and clinical training in music therapy are based on professional standards according to cultural, social, and political contexts.
> (www.wfmt.info/WFMT/About_WFMT.html)

Their website also includes the statements that 'we believe music has the power to heal and promote well-being', and 'we advocate for the use of music therapy to promote equity, social justice, and peaceful resolution'.

Music therapy seems to be effective in a wide range of contexts and life stages. Haslbeck (2012), for instance, reports on the results of studies with pre-term babies in neonatal care and their mothers. For such babies, the perfect intra-uterine world of swishing sounds, steady heartbeats and mother's voice is replaced by the stressful acoustics of an intensive-care ward. Recorded auditory stimulation was the most common intervention, including sung or instrumental lullabies, or the mother's heartbeat, but some studies used the mother's live singing. In some cases, a 'breathing bear' was added to the crib, adjusted to breathe at the same rate as the infant, and the baby could self-regulate the intervention by making contact with the bear. Almost all studies showed positive results, with the only warning being of the potential danger of over-stimulation; the most effective were those in which the baby had some measure of control.

At the other end of life, McConnell and Porter (2017) summarise the evidence for the effectiveness of music therapy in palliative-care patients, concluding that music therapy may be an effective non-pharmacological approach to managing their distressing symptoms, including reducing pain, depression and nausea, and improving mood and well-being. The techniques include listening to music, making music using instrumental or vocal performance or improvisation, songwriting and recording, often to leave a legacy, analysis of song lyrics, and musical entrainment – matching music to a patient's mood and then changing aspects such as tempo towards desirable therapeutic goals.

Although these reviews 'bookend' the uses of music therapy throughout life, many studies investigate its effectiveness in a wide range of contexts; a handbook (Edwards, 2016) includes chapters on music therapy interventions with patients who are suffering from cancer, eating disorders, traumatic brain injury, autism, dementia, and even hearing loss. The music utilised can be in the form of listening to recordings, performance of existing music, composing entirely new works, or creating music by improvisation. In some cases, as in the breathing bears, the music consists of appropriate soundscapes.

It seems undeniable that music in a therapeutic mode can have a positive effect on individuals, but music therapy also has a strong connection to social sustainability as it carries out its beneficial work on multiple individuals, on family and community groups, and on society as a whole. As an example, consider Zarate's (2016) theoretical investigation of the role of music therapy in anxiety. She points out that anxiety is a relational, multisensory and embodied experience that has its roots in competitive individualism, power imbalances, and differential privilege. As anxiety is a social construct, therapy needs to include the social dimension. Music-making in community contexts is a powerful way of increasing social agency and addressing key symptoms of anxiety by investigating their impact on individual and group empowerment. There is an obvious contrast here between treating symptoms of anxiety in an individual patient and working for change of the causes of anxiety in the whole society. As the author states in her conclusion, 'An anxiety and music therapy theory has potential to better identify and define anxiety within our convergent culture'.

Indeed, some approaches to music therapy include an essential component of advocating for social change. Curtis's (2016) investigation of the role of music therapy with women who have experienced domestic violence is based on a feminist approach to music therapy. This approach explicitly aims 'to accomplish personal transformation by individuals within their own lives and sociopolitical change within the community' (p. 296). Musical activities such as analysis of lyrics, songwriting, performance and recording, and improvisatory drumming are utilised to bypass the verbal aspects of such negative experience, and promote a music-centred relaxation and self-nurturing. In parallel to this, feminist analysis of power and gender, women's empowerment, and valuing of women's perspectives contributes to a fundamental change in social dynamics.

There is much evidence that music is a health resource for individuals and also for society as a whole. A study carried out by Saarikallio et al. (2020) investigated the psychological health benefits of music in the lives of Scandinavian music professionals – teachers, therapists, musicians, and academics. Almost all the musicians claimed that music was beneficial to their health, although the academics were less positive than the other groups, with affective experiences, belonging, and mood regulation identified as the most useful functions. This is in contrast with the general Danish population, who identified relaxation and concentration as the most useful functions of music. It is interesting that music can be a profession and a health resource at the same time for a group of professionals in society.

Changing Society With Music

Aspects of social sustainability range from the well-being of individual members of society through to the well-being of society itself – the political structure, social infrastructure, social coherence, and governance of society as a whole. While the previous sections have been concerned with individuals or groups of people, this section focuses on the government and politics of society. What role does music play in this process of social sustainability on the largest scale? How does music contribute to societal change when the conditions of society are in need of improvement – either through a process of steady incremental change, or through more dramatic revolutionary changes?

Firstly, some important questions need to be considered. How can members of a society decide (and agree on) what sort of society they need? Who decides what sort of society should be kept and what should be replaced? What prompts a decision that societal change is needed – and in particular, revolutionary change? The response to such questions necessarily involves value judgements. The notion of social sustainability includes values such as equity and social justice, increase in participation and social cohesion, and widespread engagement in the processes of social governance. Such a stance recognises that the change in South African society represented by the dismantling of the apartheid system in the 1990s was a positive one, and the change in German society resulting in the rise of Nazism in the 1930s was a negative one. Social sustainability places greater value on government and political conditions that enable society to move towards a culture that places more value on sustainability in all its forms.

Music can promote the values of 'liberty, equality, and fraternity', as in the period following the French Revolution of 1789 with songs such as 'La Marseillaise'. This prototypical revolutionary anthem was an easy way to spread the message in a largely illiterate population. However, music can be used to control social behaviour towards solidarity for a specific in-group, and hostility towards others. The 'model plays' (*yangbanxi*) of China's Cultural Revolution of 1966–1976 prescribed ideal proletarian behaviour. Operas such as *Taking Tiger Mountain by Strategy* told of the struggle and ultimate victory of heroic peasants, workers, and soldiers against bourgeois and capitalist enemies (Luo, 2018). At its extreme, music can be used to manipulate attitudes and behaviour towards the unethical. The fascist movement that developed in Germany in the 1930s utilised musical propaganda such as the Horst Wessel song in just this way. Essentially, a value judgement has to be made that certain types of social organisation are more likely to move society towards one that is sustainable in all aspects.

One example of incremental social change was the role of music in increasing opposition to the US involvement in Vietnam during the 1960s. For the most part, this opposition was developed through popular song, protest music that was a way of publicising alternative viewpoints and challenging the hegemony of government-controlled journalism (Lee, 2009). Such music was widely disseminated at coffee house meetings, marches and demonstrations, and live concerts to a mostly young audience. Early songs such as Bob Dylan's 'Blowin' in the Wind' (1963) presented general anti-war messages, at a time when the US government was claiming that they only had 'advisors' in Vietnam – 16,000 of them. Later songs such as John Lennon's 'Give Peace a Chance' (1969) were more explicit, and performances drew on the social power of unison singing. The Woodstock Rock Festival in 1969 made a significant contribution to the message of peace. A highlight was rock guitarist, Jimi Hendrix, playing the American national anthem, 'The Star-Spangled Banner', with electronically manipulated and distorted guitar sounds painting a realistic sound picture of war itself. Overall, music played a significant role in strengthening anti-war sentiment during the 1960s and ultimately ending US involvement in the Vietnam War in 1973.

A more sudden social change was the Singing Revolution, the Estonian independence movement of 1988–1991. Waren (2012) points out that this was a unique example of the role of music in a peaceful social movement in the face of military aggression. Although Estonia was occupied for most of its history, with only a short period of independence from 1918 to 1940 between the two world wars, its language and culture – particularly musical culture – enabled it to keep a strong sense of identity. Song festivals were a strong expression of social unity, with traditional songs sung by choirs of tens of thousands. Environmental protests in the late 1980s morphed into independence protests, supported by newly composed songs such as Alo Mattisen's 'Ei ole üksi ükski maa' ('No Country is Alone'). Three music festivals in 1988, the third attended by more than one-fifth of the Estonian population, gathered overwhelming support for independence, and a declaration was signed into law. The following year, the Baltic Way, a 600 km human chain from Tallinn (Estonia) to Riga (Latvia) to Vilnius (Lithuania), presented a show of unity, and in 1991 the Soviet Union formally recognised the independence of all three Baltic countries. Music and musicians played an integral role in the process, particularly by strengthening national identity through song and song festivals.

While there is nothing inherently political or revolutionary about music, every social movement or revolution has its own music, as the examples in this section indicate. Music seems to have the power to announce or even predict significant social change, incremental or revolutionary. Looking to the contemporary situation, the most serious problems are concerned with the changing of the earth's climate. While these are undoubtedly environmental problems, they are also problems of social sustainability. Musicians and other artists have an essential role in convincing people, particularly politicians, that climate change is a problem, clarifying the various aspects of the problem and envisaging ways in which social change can lead to solutions. Music, and particularly the widespread participation in musical activities, has an essential role in building social structures and values that can move society towards sustainable ways of living. A transition towards a 'culture of sustainability' (Wolcott, 2016) is the next revolution.

7 Case Studies of Music and Sustainability

Introduction

The case studies of the previous four chapters have focused in turn on the connections between music and each of the 'four pillars of sustainability' – cultural, environmental, economic, and social. The current chapter broadens this idea by presenting three particular areas of music viewed from each of the four pillars. These case studies are designed to support the thesis that whatever musical area or topic is selected, it can be related to environmental, social, economic, and cultural sustainability to some extent. Readers are challenged to pick some other area or topic of music and treat it in the same way – investigate the environmental, social, economic, and cultural aspects of sustainability in the context of their particular example. When this can be done successfully, consideration of sustainability in the context of music has moved to the broadest mode of action, as discussed in Chapter 2. It is far beyond the 'disparate', where sustainability and music are viewed as completely separate activities, beyond the 'overlapping', where sustainability can be a source of examples in areas of music, to the 'integrated', where sustainability is seen as an essential, inseparable aspect of music.

The first case study explores the area of 'early music', commonly viewed as music of the Renaissance or Baroque, which may be expanded to include other musical periods and specific contexts. At its broadest, early music represents a particular view of music, an approach in which the historical, social, and cultural context forms a basis for developing an informed contemporary performance. Various examples are used to highlight the cultural, environmental, economic, and social aspects of early music, based initially on the 'resources' view of sustainability, and then expanded to illustrate the 'justice' view in the context of a cross-cultural project set in Bolivia.

The second case study looks at the musical phenomenon of creolisation – the blending and combining of music from distinctly different roots to create new musical cultures. Although the term 'creolisation' is relatively

DOI: 10.4324/9781003044642-7

recent, the process that it represents has a long history. The combination of African musical traditions and European classical music that created jazz may be the most famous example historically, and it can be used to provide connections with each of the 'four pillars of sustainability'. The contemporary context of ever-increasing numbers of people from diverse cultural backgrounds, living in larger cities results in many examples of creolisation derived from urban popular music.

The final case study investigates aspects of sustainability in the context of Australian Indigenous music. This is an important case study for us as Australian authors. We live in a country that has been inhabited for tens of thousands of years by our Indigenous peoples, whose integrated view of sustainability has been a continuing core value. Their custodianship of the land has ensured its environmental sustainability over this immense time span, their music and art have played a central role in ensuring cultural and social sustainability, and ethical allocation of resources has avoided problems of economic sustainability. The disruptions to Indigenous society over the previous 250 years have corresponded to the rise of problems of sustainability, culminating in the current crisis. We believe that the knowledge, experience, example, and world-view of indigenous peoples, in Australia and other parts of the world, can make an important contribution to addressing, mitigating, and perhaps even solving these problems.

Early Music

The whole idea of early music is a relatively recent phenomenon, an essentially modernist endeavour particularly focused on Western classical music. In earlier ages, musicians played the music of their own times and surroundings, whether it was folk music, church music, or classical music. A rare early exception was the original Academy of Ancient Music, founded in London in 1726 for the purposes of studying and performing 'ancient' music, defined as 'music composed more than 20 years earlier' (according to the website of its modern revival, at www.aam.co.uk). It is only since the early 20th century, with the pioneering efforts of musicians such as Arnold Dolmetsch (1858–1940) and Wanda Landowska (1879–1959), that musicians have become involved with playing music that is different from the music of their own time and place.

The term 'early music' can mean different things to different musicians. Its most straightforward application is to music from earlier historical periods, most commonly the Renaissance and the Baroque. A broader interpretation views early music as the music of an identifiable previous setting, genre, place, or context. This adds further musical periods, such as medieval or Romantic music into consideration. It also incorporates specific examples, for instance, the 21 piano Nocturnes of Frédéric Chopin, written between 1827 and 1846. The common term 'historically informed performance' (or HIP) is particularly appropriate for this view of early music, as musicians investigate the historical and social background of such music and use this to construct convincing performances that reflect the conditions of the times. The broadest interpretation of early music is as a way of thinking about music beyond particular musical periods and even beyond particular settings or contexts. Early music is an approach to music and a state of mind that can apply to any music or musician, from a medieval Spanish chant to a 20th-century quartet for bamboo pipes. The HIP acronym is recast as 'historically informed practice', or even abbreviated to IP, 'informed practice', in the current discourse around research-led musical practice (Reid et al., 2021).

In terms of cultural sustainability, the most immediate aspect of early music is that it safeguards the cultural heritage of earlier times, the music itself as well as the social and cultural conditions in which it was created and played. This can be considered in general terms, as in the heritage of Renaissance music and culture, or in more restricted terms, such as the recreation of the colonial musical culture of early Sydney, based on the Dowling Songbook, a collection of sheet music for voice and piano bound together in 1840 and annotated by a wealthy colonial couple, Lilias and Willoughby Dowling (Yeadon, 2021, and www.youtube.com/watch?v=qaYcgQsbct8&feature=youtu.be). It can also be applied to quite specific contexts, such as the Ottoman music available in late 18th-century London, as shown by the tunes built into a mechanical organ-clock of the day, an early example of exotic music that survives in 'recorded' form (Banks & Lefeber, 2018). In each example, general to specific, early music as a whole is responsible for the sustainability of musical cultures from past times and places.

In terms of environmental sustainability, an obvious concern is the materials from which early instruments are constructed. Early flutes were made using woods such as boxwood (some were even made from ivory or porcelain), stringed instruments were strung with animal gut, brass instruments were constructed from metal tubes, and harpsichords were built using an array of special woods, leather quills, metal strings, and ivory keys. In contemporary times, copies of original instruments are often made with similar materials (with the exclusion of ivory). While the makers of the original instruments had few environmental pressures on their materials, the situation is quite different now, exacerbated by the much larger numbers of instruments being made for a much greater population. Some materials are restricted, such as rosewood or ebony wood for flutes, while others can be substituted, such as Asian boxwood for European boxwood, or nylon (Nylgut) for gut strings. Other materials have been completely replaced, such as the ivory that was used for the accidental keys of harpsichords, now replaced by bone or plastics. This is only one of the connections between early music and environmental sustainability.

Turning to the aspect of economic sustainability, it is apparent that the early music revival has led to a growth of professional groups specialising in various aspects of early music. An Australian example is the Sydney-based Pinchgut Opera (www.pinchgutopera.com.au), that has for almost two decades presented performances of early opera, by well-known composers such as Handel and Vivaldi, but also by lesser-known names such as Grétry and Cavalli. Another example is the Canadian early orchestra and choir Tafelmusik (www.tafelmusik.org), specialising in performances of music from the 17th to the 19th century, played on period instruments and based on the latest scholarship. Tafelmusik also maintains a regular Canadian and international touring programme (an activity that has aspects of environmental as well as economic sustainability), and both groups have created digital programmes during the 2020 Covid-19 pandemic. Such groups contribute to the economic aspects of early music, with their artistic activities, performances, and recordings, and hence to the economic sustainability of the community.

Finally, the aspects of early music most relevant to social sustainability concern the large group of people who make up the 'early music movement'. There is a worldwide interest in early music, most obviously from amateur musicians who play early instruments individually or in ensembles, participate in workshops and classes, belong to early music societies, or are simply regular attendees at early music concerts and exhibitions. The many social and personal benefits of participating in live music have been discussed earlier (in Chapter 6). Music played by amateur consorts of recorders or viols, or sung in amateur madrigal groups and choirs, generally mirrors earlier times when people created their own entertainment. There were professional players and ensembles in courts, churches, and cities. However, while there is a certain amount of early music aimed at the professional level, there is also a large amount that is written at a standard that is accessible to good amateur players, leading to an appreciable contribution of early music to social sustainability.

The points mentioned so far can all be seen as examples of the 'resources' conception of sustainability – cultural, biological, economic, and social resources. The final example expands this to the 'justice' conception. The Bolivian project was undertaken by Ashley Solomon and the British period ensemble Florilegium (www.florilegium.org.uk/bolivian-diary/). They worked with local Bolivian musicians to bring back to life the Baroque music taken to South America by the Jesuits in the mid-17th century for music-making on their missions. The European music taken to Bolivia was

76   Case Studies of Music and Sustainability

augmented by other compositions by the local people. When the Jesuits were expelled from Bolivia in 1767, the missions were closed and their music libraries of many thousands of works were placed in storage. In 2002, Florilegium accepted an invitation to participate in a Bolivian music festival and to include some of this Bolivian Baroque music in their programme.

The collaboration that developed resulted in further exploration of the repertoire, preparation and performance of various pieces in concerts in Bolivia and internationally, and three recordings of the repertoire. At each stage in the process, local musicians were first supported in their training, and then included in concerts and tours both as singers and instrumentalists, and ultimately also as composers. These musicians were, of course, descendants of the original participants, who gave, and still give, an indigenous component to this originally European music. Their inclusion in the project results in performances of a particular style, arguably more authentic recreations of the original 17th-century music-making, but with an overlay of Bolivian exuberance and joy.

The Jesuits aimed to protect Bolivian culture while at the same time trying to convert indigenous Bolivian people to Christianity. Florilegium's Bolivian project has revived and rebalanced the cultural heritage of a body of European and Bolivian music that was thought to have been lost. One review on their website refers to it as a 'really remarkable musical "fair-trade" product'. The vital collaboration between musicians of different cultural backgrounds presents a fascinating example of sustainability and early music at the broadest, 'justice' level.

Musical Creolisation

Originally, the term 'creole' referred to a person of mixed European and local (particularly Caribbean) descent, or the language formed by contact between European and local languages. Creolisation is the process of mixing cultures, of utilising aspects of different cultures in combination. The term was originally applied to late 20th century analysis of Caribbean culture's mix of indigenous, African, and European elements, particularly languages. The current broader notion is the development of a new culture from a combination of traditional ones, and it includes the combining and blending of musical cultures. Creolisation is a valuable concept for broadening the understanding of music for cultural heritage and sustainability.

Musicians have always used the combination of different cultural elements as a source of inspiration for their composing and performing. An example from the Renaissance is Orlando di Lasso's *Allala pia calia*, a composition using an unusual dialect and nonsense Italian words to caricature the Moorish domestic servants of wealthy Neapolitans (www.youtube.com/watch?v=aVxRTx13C38). Indeed, the 'moresca' was a component of many dance music collections of the Renaissance, referring to the Arab (Moorish) musical influence from southern Spain. The term and the character survive in contemporary British Morris dancing.

When the young Johann Sebastian Bach was employed at the Weimar court in the early 1700s, he transcribed a number of concertos by Vivaldi and other Italian composers for keyboard instruments as a means of becoming familiar with the Italian style, and particularly the Italian concerto. This could be seen as another early example of creolisation, leading to the mixing of Italian and German (and other) styles in Bach's mature musical works. Jean-Philippe Rameau's opera *Les Indes Gallantes* (*The Amorous Indies*) sets the fourth act, *Les Sauvages* (*The Savages*), amongst the 'Indians' of North America. The famous *Danse du grand calumet de la paix* (*The great peace-pipe dance*) is inspired by a performance in Paris in 1725 given by visiting members of Illinois tribes, including Chief Chicagou, and is an example of creolisation based on contemporary interest in the exotic. Mozart's famous *Rondo Alla Turca* in his Piano Sonata No. 11 (K. 331) imitates the sound of Turkish music, particularly the Janissary military bands, much in vogue at the time. It is just one example of the creolisation of Turkish and European music in the late 18th century.

While these older and more recent historical examples of creolisation show the basic features of combining disparate musical cultures into new ones, the contemporary situation takes the notion much further. In today's globalised and digitised world, anyone with an internet connection and a streaming subscription has immediate access to almost all of the world's music, past and present. Further, while the earth's population is growing fast, almost 8 billion currently and projected to reach 10 billion in 2050, a greater proportion of people are living in urban areas than ever before; currently 55% of people, projected to increase to 68% by 2050. An increasing number and proportion of people live in cities, growing with waves of immigration often from other countries, and particularly open to musical creolisation. In such a milieu, musicians can present music from their own particular culture, they can collaborate with musicians from other cultures, or they can mix and combine different musical cultures. And in a highly competitive urban environment, commercial advantage often follows from the novelty of crossover genres developed in this way.

Petocz et al. (2014) discuss the implications for professional work of musicians. 'In essence, the music making typically found in urban settings is "creolised" – musicians combine and build upon their own and others' cultural heritages. Understanding how musicians work within such a complex environment may provide insights into the cultural health of a society and shed light on the nature of musical work' (p. 5). The Sydney-based group Lime Cordiale, led by brothers, Oliver and Louis Leimbach, was amongst the 2020 Australian Recording Industry Awards (ARIA) winners with its second album *14 Steps to a Better You*. A review (Leeson, 2020) describes the album as 'a summery dose of indie-pop festival sunshine, coloured with celebratory drips of reggae, soul,'70s soft rock, roots and Beach Boys harmonies'.

The combination and mixing of cultures involved in creolisation can occur ethically as an acknowledged and valued contribution from each culture. In some cases, particularly where a minority or indigenous culture is appropriated by a dominant Western culture, the combination displays the colonising aspects of unequal transfer, with the minority contribution acknowledged only in passing, if at all. However, that does not have to be the case. Paul Simon's album *Graceland* was inspired by the sounds of *mbaqanga*, South African township music, and combined an eclectic range of musical influences, including the Ladysmith Black Mambazo vocal group. The various cultural contributions to the album were clearly acknowledged, both in the text and financially, resulting in an ethically defensible creolisation and Simon's most successful album.

In the Australian context, creolisation can often be seen in the combination of Indigenous and European musics. One recent and successful example is the opera *Jandamarra – Sing for the Country (Ngalanybarra Muwayi.u)*, a close co-operation between the Bunuba people of the Kimberley region of Western Australia, composer Paul Stanhope, and librettist Steve Hawke. The work tells of Jandamarra, a Bunuba man whose role as a fighter against white pastoralist expansion became a Bunuba resistance story. The opera includes Bunuba music, sung in Bunuba language and played (on didjeridu) by Bunuba people, who remain the cultural owners of the Jandamarra story (and the only people allowed to sing it). A stage version of the story was produced in Perth in 2008, and the opera performed in the Sydney Opera House in 2014. A second version of the opera was presented by the Sydney Conservatorium of Music and Bunuba Cultural Enterprises in the Sydney Town Hall in 2019 and the full recording is available on the website (www.jandamarra.com.au/index.html#home).

The product of creolisation, what emerges from the combination of musical idioms and ideas, can be something completely new, a new style, movement, or idea that is more than the sum of its components. Some commentators claim that creolisation in a global context will result in homogeneity and blandness, as unique musical cultures are replaced by similar combinations worldwide; others suggest that creolisation will lead to cultural regeneration, as innovative crossover styles are developed. Both options seem possible. The widespread proliferation of 'country music' with American-accented singing of standard tropes might be an example of the former claim. The combination of Gregorian chant and jazz saxophone displayed in Jan Garbarek and the Hilliard Ensemble's *Officium* (1994), a medieval–jazz crossover, could support the latter.

Perhaps the best-known example of creolisation is the music of jazz, originally an amalgamation of African folk music and European classical music elements. The mixing has continued in reverse as elements of jazz have been incorporated into mainstream Western musical forms. Well-known examples are George Gershwin's *Rhapsody in Blue* (1924) for solo piano and jazz band, Igor Stravinsky's *Ebony Concerto* (1945), written for the clarinettist Woody Herman and his band, and Harrison Birtwistle's *Panic* (1995) featuring saxophone and jazz drum kit. Jazz itself has continued growing, incorporating diverse influences from other musical cultures, such as the gypsy jazz of the 1930s and the M-Base jazz of the 1980s.

Jazz is also a convenient context to indicate the contribution of creolisation to the various aspects of sustainability. Cultural sustainability is at the forefront as the component musical cultures are combined into novel styles of jazz that become part of contemporary and future musical culture. The environmental aspect of sustainability is highlighted by jazz compositions that focus on environmental problems, such as Sandy Evans' *Postcards from the Anthropocene* album, recorded during the Australian bushfire crisis of 2019, which 'ponders the most dangerous threat to human survival: climate change' (https://sandyevans.com.au/event/postcards-from-the-anthropocene/). The album was launched during the 2020 Sydney International Women's Jazz Festival, a reminder of the social sustainability of jazz in its appearance in many festivals (this particular one online due to the Covid-19 pandemic), and also in bars and clubs across the world. The economic aspects of sustainability are linked with jazz's widespread popularity, supporting jobs, recordings, and performances of a large group of musicians.

Essentially, these aspects of sustainability occur together in the cultural melange that is summarised by the term 'creolisation'. While such mixing has always been a part of musical creation and performance, it plays an increasingly larger role in the contemporary urban music scene of the 21st century, where many diverse musical cultures coexist and continue to inspire novel combinations. By analogy, the process of creolisation also encourages thinking about, and experimentation with, novel combinations of ideas and strategies to confront sustainability challenges of the early 21st century. This has been discussed by various authors as the 'transition to a culture of sustainability' (Wolcott, 2016), one possible path towards addressing the problems of sustainability.

Australian Indigenous Music

Aboriginal people have lived in Australia for at least 65,000 years, and they represent one of the oldest continuous cultures in history. They have lived in every part of the continent, from the driest and hottest desert lands to the coldest mountain regions and everything in between. Throughout this time, they have had a sophisticated social and cultural life in which music played an essential role. In the late 18th century, before significant European contact, the population was estimated at around 750,000 people, comprising several hundred social groupings (https://aiatsis.gov.au/explore/map-indigenous-australia) and numerous distinct languages (https://gambay.com.au/languages/).

The British invasion of 1788 was disastrous for Aboriginal society in many ways. As well as appropriation of their lands, many Indigenous people died at the hands of the invaders and settlers, or from introduced diseases. For much of the following 250 years, Indigenous people were discriminated against and mistreated by the European majority, and it is only in more recent times that the situation has begun to improve. In a referendum in 1967 Aboriginal people were granted citizenship (of their own country!). In 1973, the Canberra Aboriginal 'Tent Embassy' was acknowledged by Prime Minister Gough Whitlam, and the Aboriginal Land Rights Commission was established. In 1992, the Mabo Decision of the High Court struck down the legal doctrine of 'terra nullius' and led to the establishment of the Native Title Act 1993. In 2008, Kevin Rudd, Prime Minister of Australia, delivered a historic apology to the Stolen Generations, Indigenous children forcibly removed from their families by earlier government policies. In 2017, a national meeting of Indigenous leaders created the Uluru Statement from the Heart, calling for a formal treaty with the government and a First Nations Voice enshrined in the Constitution – this is a work still in progress. Throughout this time, despite sometimes dreadful conditions, Aboriginal society and culture have continued to show a deep resilience and, more recently, to thrive.

With this background, it is possible to point to some specific examples of intersections between Australian Indigenous music and the various aspects of sustainability. Illustrating the 'resources' conception of cultural sustainability, Campbell (2013) writes about the Kulama instruction ceremonies of the Tiwi Islands just north of Darwin. Historically, these ceremonies were components in a ritual system of graded instruction as an initiation into Tiwi culture. The Kulama relied heavily on improvisatory composition in the traditional Tiwi language, with all members of society participating. With the cultural disruptions caused by the arrival of the Catholic Mission, the system of Kulama declined. Currently, only a small number of the oldest people are holders of this traditional knowledge, and they are working to keep the cultural heritage alive. 'Elders are using repatriated ethnographic recordings as a teaching tool; not only to preserve the cultural and spiritual knowledge held in the old song texts, but also as linguistic and melodic source material for new ways of composing' (p. 237).

As in any culture, some song serves more immediate purposes. 'Wanji-wanji' is a travelling song, popular in the first half of the 20th century. Its history, travel and cultural survival is documented by The University of Sydney's Paradisec project (at https://wanji-wanji-music.sydney.edu.au/wanji-wanji-story-map/) with maps and sound recordings of the song's travels, and interviews with Indigenous people remembering it from their youth.

In terms of environmental sustainability, Ryan (2016) investigates the Indigenous musicalisation of eucalypts, via termite-hollowed branches (didjeridus, or *yidaki* in Yolngu language) and gum-leaves – both instruments capable of a sophisticated range of musical sounds. She does not mention other Indigenous instruments that are made of eucalypt (or other) woods, such as the bull-roarer, clapsticks and boomerangs (used as percussion instruments), although her arguments would apply just as well to them. Ryan discusses the connection between the eucalypts that supply musical instruments and the people who make and use the instruments; together they form a close 'social-ecological' system. The resilience of the eucalypts to environmental changes is reflected in a corresponding resilience of the musicians and musical traditions that depend on them. However, the use of eucalypts in musicking is under increased threat from anthropogenic climate change, and this in turn threatens the related music-making.

Economic sustainability is addressed by the empowerment of Indigenous musicians to create a living drawing inspiration from the artistic aspects of their culture. While visual arts have made the greatest economic contribution to Indigenous artists and communities, there is a growing interest in Indigenous music – both traditional and popular. Maybe the most famous (and commercially successful) band is Yothu Yindi, formed in 1986, with both Indigenous and non-Indigenous members, and including several members of the Yunupingu family. The group's most famous track, *Treaty*, was the first song in any Aboriginal language (Gumatj, one of the Yolngu Matha dialects) to get international recognition and commercial success. The group sponsored the Yothu Yindi Foundation, producing, since 1999, the annual Garma Festival of Traditional Cultures, estimated to contribute almost A$10 million annually to the economy of Australia's Northern Territory. There are many other Indigenous musicians and groups forging careers based on their Indigenous music. One example is the Ripple Effect Band (www.ripple-effect-band.com/), an all-women rock band from Maningrida in Arnhem Land, Northern Territory, who sing in five Aboriginal languages and use contemporary music to express cultural knowledge and negotiate their identity as women.

The most important music-making in Australian Indigenous communities takes the form of participatory group singing, indicating the key role that music plays in social sustainability. Naina Sen's film *The Song Keepers* documents the Central Australian Aboriginal Women's Choir, a group of singers from various remote community choirs, as they tour in Germany singing old Lutheran hymns taught to their forebears four generations earlier by the German missionaries in the late 1800s. Ford (2018) points out that the hymns are not simply returned to their original country. They are sung now in the Arrente and Pitjantjatjara languages, with a distinct timbre and texture, transformed by their 150 years with the Indigenous communities. The film itself refers many times to the importance of singing in the social and cultural lives of the choir members. One of the youngest singers, Heather, reflects on her decision to participate: 'It just made me feel happy that I was joining in the choir. It did really change my life. The choir, the hymns, the stages, it made me think that this was my future'.

This last example suggests that it is not so easy or reasonable to separate the four aspects of sustainability in the Indigenous context. Is the choral singing of old hymns an instance of social sustainability or is it more accurately described as the cultural sustainability not only of the Lutheran missionaries but also of the Indigenous cultural practices that were able to include a different form of song in their scope? Indeed, traditional Indigenous culture seems to be built on a holistic approach to sustainability in all its aspects.

Writing about Noongar song – from the south-west of Western Australia – from his viewpoint as a Noongar man and an academic ethnomusicologist, Bracknell (2017) points out that song is a vital part of Noongar culture. Traditionally, song was as common as speech, as a means of communication and maintenance of shared collective memory, a historical repository constantly updated, and a source of geographical and spiritual information about country. There is an interdependent connection between song and land; singing country into life leads to country caring for its inhabitants. Noongar songs sustain the Dreaming, a simplistic translation of a foundational Aboriginal concept that 'involves manifestations of ancestral beings as the physical landscape, as the social and ecological order that the ancestors created, and as animals, plants, or natural features, such as wind and fire' (p. 102).

This essential relationship between people, ancestral creators, and land seems to be a feature of Australian Indigenous cultures generally, manifest in Songlines – invisible, interconnected routes, signposted in song, that mark significant sites and map the paths between them. 'They provide a complex Aboriginal knowledge system to educate our people of their country and entire world, beginning with their land and a belief system, sustaining not only their physical world but more importantly their spiritual realm' (Perry & Holt, 2018). Indigenous knowledge is contained and summarised in music in a holistic manner that does not distinguish between the cultural, the environmental, the economic, or the social. There is a significant lesson here for sustainability.

8 Conclusion

Looking Backwards – And Forwards

This book investigates relationships and intersections between music and sustainability. The basic question for a musician, a music teacher, or a music student is simply 'What does music have to do with sustainability?' Chapter 1 introduced the idea that music and sustainability are vitally connected, and that music has a key role in addressing problems of sustainability. It presented the view that music – and art in general – is a powerful way of thinking, knowing, researching, and being. In particular, music is a way of imagining and developing sustainable ways of living. That chapter gave evidence from three different cultures, ancient and modern, about the close connection between music and sustainability. Chapter 2 presented a background to early 21st-century thinking about sustainability, introducing the 'four-pillar model', in which sustainability is viewed from cultural, environmental, economic, and social aspects in turn. The central part of the book is the series of 19 case studies of intersections between specific topics in music and particular aspects of sustainability, comprising Chapters 3 to 7.

This final chapter investigates the pedagogical dimension of these ideas. At its most fundamental, learning in music is concerned with the process of developing broader views and understandings of music itself and its role in life. The discussion in this book focuses on the role of music in life, and specifically in the features of life that are concerned with aspects of sustainability. This chapter explores how these case studies can be used pedagogically by musicians, music educators, and music students to give practical form to the ideas, and to make themselves and their colleagues, audiences, and students more aware of the music and sustainability nexus. It presents suggestions to develop ways of learning and teaching music, of working as a musician, and of becoming and being a professional or community musician able to play their part in the discussion, debate, and action needed to face the crisis of sustainability in the early 21st century.

DOI: 10.4324/9781003044642-8

Curriculum for Music Education

Music is, at least potentially, a lifelong part of people's experience. Much of learning and practising music occurs informally, outside any educational system. However, it is in the formal music education system that people come to decide and define what music is, what it means to them, and to what extent they will participate in it for the rest of their lives. Music curriculum at the school level is an important input into people's thinking about music. Music curriculum at the university or conservatorium level is important for the future musical life and work of the small proportion of people who will become professional musicians, including teachers of music, who with their musical practice will model the range of ideas about music for the rest of society.

There is a large variety of music curricula in different educational systems, and the details are not of concern here. However, it is useful to discuss two extremes of curriculum for music education, that might be referred to as 'narrow' and 'broad'. A narrow curriculum focuses on the elements of music – rhythm, pitch, harmony, technique, and so on – that are deemed to be important in order to learn the language of music and to practise music as a performer or to create music as a composer. Such a curriculum can teach a person much about music, from its beginnings to its professional practice. But a narrow curriculum remains inward looking, focused on the music itself and the technical aspects of reading, performing, or creating it. One side effect of such a curriculum is that some people – maybe many – will decide that they have little talent for music and interest in the subject, and will limit, and maybe even curtail their engagement with music.

A broad curriculum, by contrast, includes but goes well beyond the technical elements. Such a curriculum looks outwards from a musical centre, focuses on the use of music as a way of thinking and communicating, an approach to life, an inclusive tool to investigate, and even change the world. A broad curriculum approaches music as an essential part of living for all people, at all ages, and with all levels of musical ability. It continually investigates inter-relationships between music and other facets of life, and situates music in a social, intellectual, and cultural context. Very few people will turn their backs on music if it is presented in such a broad way, in the same way that very few people will ignore reading and writing as modes of communicating and living. It is important to note that a broad curriculum does not ignore the basic musical elements and techniques, but rather, uses them as a starting point from which the subject of music can expand.

The narrow music curriculum is identified and described as an extreme. It is not common that music education at any level consists solely of such components and technical aspects. Yet, elements of such an approach to music education can be found in many contexts, from examinations of basic skills in music theory at beginner level to the preparation of a virtuoso solo piano étude by an advanced student in a conservatorium. Such aspects are a necessary part of music learning, but for most effective music education they need to be set in a broader context, where the relationships between music and other aspects of life are identified and acknowledged. In particular, as this book argues, the relationship between music and sustainability provides a valuable framework where the cultural, environmental, social, and economic aspects of music can be investigated in the relevant context of the contemporary problems of sustainability.

The aspirations of the UN's Decade of Education for Sustainable Development (DESD, 2005–2014) were to integrate sustainability into education at all levels and in all disciplines. These were ambitious targets, and still represent an important 'work in progress' nearly a decade later. Music has the advantage of obvious intersections with cultural sustainability, not only in specific sub-disciplines such as ethnomusicology, but more broadly by considering that any music is a reflection of the cultural conditions of its time. The case studies in this book present a range of examples of relationships between various topics in music and aspects of environmental, economic and social, as well as cultural, sustainability. Using a broad curriculum approach, in more explicit interdisciplinary settings, they can continue the work of the DESD. The current focus in many Western education systems on STEM subjects – science, technology, engineering, and mathematics – can be usefully broadened to STEAM, integrating the creativity, vision, and social awareness of art, including music, to the scientific and quantitative mix of STEM (Taylor, 2016).

One important feature of a broad curriculum is that it encourages people towards the broadest ideas about dispositions such as sustainability. Our previous research on *conceptions of sustainability* was presented in Chapter 2. The three conceptions – the narrowest 'distance' view, the intermediate 'resources' view, and the broadest 'justice' view – are hierarchical; the broader views build on the narrower views by adding more understandings. Each of the conceptions is associated with a way of behaving, which we labelled 'disparate', 'overlapping', and 'integrated'. In the context of music, a person with a 'distance' view of sustainability is limited to 'disparate' ways of behaving, focusing on their music and viewing sustainability as an unrelated idea. A person with a 'resources' view of sustainability is able to make use of 'overlapping' actions to find and investigate intersections between their music and the ideas of sustainability. And a musician who understands the 'justice' view of sustainability can use 'integrated' ways of behaving to identify essential relationships between music and sustainability and consider their effects, including ethical aspects, on the individuals and groups

Conclusion 87

involved. Working with a broad curriculum in music encourages teachers and students towards broader views of sustainability and so towards broader ways of enacting sustainability in their musicking. The case studies in the previous chapters have highlighted wherever possible the 'justice' view of sustainability, supported by references to the 'resources' view.

Beginning to Learn Music for Sustainability

Learning in music occurs from the moment a child starts to listen to the sounds made by their parents. From the outset, sound, speech, and music are contextualised for the infant. Awareness of variation in aspects of the world is the precursor for learning at any level or age. As an infant notices variation in the tones coming from nearby adults she learns to discern and imitate those that are important in particular contexts. Noticing how some feature of the world around them is different from some other feature, or some sound is different from another sound, is the first step in understanding the feature or sound, and then making use of it.

Shevock (2015) opens his discussion of 'the possibility of eco-literate music pedagogy' with a description of what could be considered one of his son's first music lessons – at the age of eight months. He describes taking him to a remote part of a city park, sitting on the grass under some trees, and listening to the 'music of the park', nature's music, a learning experience for both son and father. He concludes his paper by deciding that 'music education has the potential to provide meaningful insight into ecological crises facing the world, especially through sonic experience and ritualization . . . of ecological experiences' (p. 16). His subsequent book (Shevock, 2018), already referred to in the discussion of *ecomusicology* (Chapter 4), suggests a wide range of activities that can be used by music educators at any level to raise awareness of the essential connections between music and sustainability, particularly environmental sustainability.

Composer and art-science educator Østergaard (2019) believes that music has an essential role in education for sustainability that begins, at any age, with the act of attentive listening. His central thesis is that 'music and attentive listening have the potential of strengthening sensuous awareness and world engagement, two essential elements of students' sustainability engagement' (p. 3). Music has 'a rich tradition of close listening and aural attendance' (p. 4) that is often missing in traditional discussions of sustainability. Children of all ages (as well as adults) can develop their listening skills to become more aware of nature's sonic expressions, and so become more 'eco-acoustically aware'. This view seems consistent with Shevock's aims for his son's informal musical education, and is also supported by Titon's (2016) discussion of the ecological writings of the 19th-century

American naturalist and philosopher Henry David Thoreau. Østergaard points out that interdisciplinary contexts, formal or informal, are the most fertile learning situations for identifying links between music and sustainability. Musical compositions in the form of soundscapes are manifestations of such links, shaped by the composer to highlight the interplay of human-made and natural sounds, and aided by the common performance convention that music should be listened to attentively.

Learning Music for Sustainability at School

Most children experience some musical education at school, although the particular details depend on the country in which they live and the specific school curriculum that applies. Generally, music classes start at the beginning of primary school. In some systems they continue all through secondary school, while in others compulsory music is replaced by elective subjects some time during secondary school. School-age students engage with music in many different ways depending on the focus of national and local curricula. In some countries, daily singing is used as a means of introducing musical elements, while in others, playing an instrument such as the recorder is used as an introduction to the written aspects of music. In some countries, music is considered an integral subject and activity, alongside language, mathematics, and science. In other countries, music education is seen as an option; something students do as an extra-curricular activity rather than being central to the curriculum. Some countries implement specialised approaches, such as the Kodály method in Hungary that allows students to learn to sight-sing confidently using their traditional folk music, added to the UNESCO *Intangible Cultural Heritage* in 2016 (Chapter 3).

The most common musical examples use the Western musical canon, particularly the music of the 18th and 19th centuries. Many countries make use of their folk music also, particularly at the earlier levels. On the whole, the curricula reflect the historical and pedagogical concerns of each country. As one example, Mack (2021) describes the dilemma of music education in Indonesia. Western art music was initially privileged due to the colonial history, but that is under reconsideration to ensure that the traditional musics of Indonesia are as strongly represented. These are complex issues, as music plays a central role in cultural understanding, and is a visible marker of the value and recognition of different aspects of cultural background. The discussion of *ethnomusicology* in Chapter 3 highlights the importance of ensuring the sustainability of different musical cultures by ensuring their survival and continued use and relevance by young people.

In the authors' own state of New South Wales, Australia, music education diminishes during public secondary schooling, leaving musical activity

Conclusion   89

for many students centred on voluntary activity in the community. Given the cost of instrumental lessons, the effect is socially disruptive as only wealthier parents can continue to provide music education for their children. However, some private schools continue with a comprehensive music programme throughout the years of secondary schooling. This provides an inequitable situation for music education, and advocacy groups from within the musical community are endlessly lobbying to ensure that music education is available for all children throughout their schooling. Music education professionals often need to become advocates for the inclusion of various forms of music within national curricula.

One common feature of school curricula is that they tend to be centrally decided and mandated, and the individual teacher has relatively little ability to vary it. The extent to which a broad music curriculum is experienced varies, but most countries incorporate some discussion of the social and cultural dimensions of music. Even in a fairly rigid curriculum context, teachers will have some room to broaden the discussions to introduce aspects of sustainability. Interdisciplinary approaches have the potential to increase such possibilities, but again teachers may be constrained by curriculum as well as practical aspects such as timetabling of lessons.

Regardless of the place of music education in specific curricula, it is important that educators take the opportunity to present music as something that is central to personal and cultural well-being. Through participation in musical activity, children learn about their society and other societies, and start to develop their personal collection of musical experiences that can be used as a basis of reflection on diverse genres. At a young age, music education also encourages the aural, spatial, and symbolic thinking that is essential for the acquisition of language and mathematics. Further, musical activity has a clear benefit for group cohesion and creative thinking. In addition, music provides an example of the benefits of collaborative working, and gives a useful counterbalance to the competitive aspects that so often predominate in school contexts.

For teachers at school, we offer the case studies in this book as examples of intersections between music and sustainability. Many of them could be used as provocative material for a discussion in a music classroom. The case study of musical *composition* linked to aspects of environmental sustainability (Chapter 4), for instance, could provide a useful introduction to a current work that the students are studying. If interdisciplinary approaches are possible, this could take place in a social science, economics, history, or science class as well as a music class, maybe after an initial discussion of the ideas of sustainability. The examples concerning the benefits of *participatory music* (Chapter 6), *the cost of music* (Chapter 5), *changing society with music* (Chapter 6), or *scaling the octave* (Chapter 3) could find a use here. Students can be challenged to debate the role of the particular feature of music in the specific aspect of sustainability in the context of the case study. They can be asked to support or oppose the argument put forward in the example. They can be encouraged to find further instances related to the example, or to develop quite different examples relating music and sustainability. They can be challenged to respond to the problem raised, or another similar problem, in some creative or artistic way. The most obvious benefit for students will be a broadening of their views of music, its role in their lives, and its links to contemporary problems. They can also benefit from experience with artistic ways of thinking and acting, and from the acknowledgement that an artistic response to a problem is a valid one.

Learning Music for Sustainability at the Conservatorium

Young people (and some older people) who have decided to study music at a conservatorium are taking a step into music at the professional level. While they are students they will engage with the full range of musical learning, theoretical and practical, that could be described by the highest and most focused levels of the narrow curriculum. They will, for instance, study harmony in great detail, maybe giving it practical form in their own arrangements or compositions, and they will improve their facility to sing or play an instrument to an expert level. They will also have opportunities to develop more generic abilities such as communication and team work, and to consider broader aspects of music, such as the nature of musical creativity, or the connections of music with current problems of sustainability. We believe that the case studies in this book could be useful examples in this endeavour; each one is supported with a small number of interesting and relevant references, selected to be at a level suitable for tertiary students.

For students commencing such a course of study, the introduction of a broad sweep of musicological ideas is a first step to understanding the complexity and variation of music in society. Often, however, musicology is set at the narrowest level, focusing, for instance, on the music of the (European) Classical and Romantic eras in a way that leaves out much of the cultural, social, historical, and scientific practice. Broadening musicology to ensure that the music featured includes examples from a larger variety of contemporary and historical societies is a means of increasing students' understanding of the contemporary context of their music-making. Such pre-professional musicians often have the possibility of listening to and playing with musicians from varied cultural backgrounds. Musics from those different backgrounds, traditional or contemporary, should be equally privileged in serious musicological discussions. The case studies on *ecomusicology* (Chapter 4) and **musical creolisation** (Chapter 7) could be useful in this context, and an example such as the opera *Jandamarra – Sing for the Country* (*Ngalanybarra Muwayi.u*) is valuable not only musicologically but also for its role in coming to terms with historical injustices.

In terms of musical performance, Western art music, particularly the music of the 'long 19th century', holds a pre-eminent position in tertiary music studies, fostered particularly through the worldwide conservatoire system. The music is undoubtedly beautiful as well as significant, and deserves to be fostered; the virtuoso performance of such music is a laudable goal for music students. However, a much wider range of musical traditions – including folk musics, indigenous musics, jazz, and contemporary popular music – deserves a role in the formal curricula of tertiary music schools. Here, the case studies on **ethnomusicology** (Chapter 3) and **early music** (Chapter 7) could be useful discussions. At the Sydney Conservatorium of Music, a thriving Chinese Music Ensemble and a Gamelan Ensemble give students opportunities to study and perform traditional music from China and Bali, Indonesia, and gain experience of their cultural background and performance styles. Other music schools will have opportunities to contribute to cultural sustainability of music from their own regions.

Quite reasonably, much of the study at a tertiary music school is focused on the music itself, both theoretically in musicology and practically in performance. This can also be broadened to include intersections with related skills and dispositions that represent aspects of professional preparation, such as business and organisational skills. The case studies on **music careers as small businesses** (Chapter 5) and **symphony orchestras and sustainability** (Chapter 6) would be relevant examples in this case. While much of the music-making in a tertiary course occurs in the context of small or large ensembles, the focus can be broadened to interdisciplinary teams, including professionals from different discipline areas to investigate a problem in social or environmental sustainability. Here the case study of **music and health** in Chapter 6 could even introduce a possible professional specialisation for music students. Indeed, including music and health in the curriculum for pre-professional musicians would have a two-fold effect, prompting the students to consider their own health through ergonomic performance practice, this for career longevity, and to develop an interest and capacity to contribute to others' health through the power of music.

Tertiary courses in music often include a specialisation in music education. Students of music education are in that liminal place where their roles as learners and teachers overlap, and where they can use the experiences of their own learning as vital resources for their own teaching. Considering the critical importance of sustainability for the future of humanity, curriculum for music education has a key role in providing future teachers with a grounding in music for sustainability. Aspects of sustainability – most obviously cultural sustainability, but also environmental, economic, and social – can be embedded in most (or all) of their units of study, as a model for their future music teaching. Music education students can be encouraged to view music as a cultural artefact, to engage with the social and environmental background of the works they study, and to consider the widest diversity of musical styles and genres. This will prepare them for their role as teachers of the next generation, able to engage with students from diverse cultural backgrounds, including, particularly in Australia, those with an Indigenous background. The case studies in this book can serve as a starting point for further investigations of different traditional and contemporary cultures. Further, they could be seen as examples of teaching materials that could be used with their own classes. Many of the case studies, for instance, could be modified to the appropriate level for class reading, supported by a short list of questions for group discussion or individual thinking and writing.

A practical means of engaging pre-professional musicians with sustainability in music is the use of 'capstone' projects in the final years of formal study. Such projects are usually chosen by students themselves, and may be based on problems identified by an external partner such as an arts organisation or a community group. This book's case studies could suggest other projects; for instance, developing the contribution of a professional music group to local social sustainability (based on *symphony orchestras and sustainability*, Chapter 6), or working with an arts organisation to minimise the environmental effects of touring (based on *touring musicians*, Chapter 4). The work of the project is carried out in student groups, often including members with different areas of expertise. A capstone project usually grapples with an important issue, maybe a 'wicked' problem – difficult to formulate as well as to solve – and the conclusion can be in a standard report format, or maybe in the form of an artistic response to the issue. Community reaction suggests that this is a legitimate form of artistic engagement with contemporary issues, and often looks extremely different from performances expected in traditional concert halls.

Enacting Sustainability as a Professional or Community Musician

Professional musicians – and artists in general – have an important role in reflecting on, and being critical of, their society, identifying current problems and behaviour that contribute to them, and suggesting alternative ways of being that can address those problems or even solve them. This is the implicit social contract between artists and the society that supports them. In particular, musicians have an artistic and social role in raising awareness of problems of sustainability, and envisioning solutions to those problems. Performers can exemplify more sustainable ways of living, and they can talk about such behaviours with their audience, as discussed in the case study of *touring musicians* (Chapter 4). Composers can raise awareness of environmental or social problems by using them as themes in their music, as demonstrated in the *composition* case study (Chapter 4). Commercial music writers can use their knowledge of the manipulative power of music used in games, movies, and advertising to influence people's thinking and behaviour towards more sustainable choices. Musicologists and music researchers can investigate the cultural heritage of groups of people, traditional or contemporary, as exemplified in the *ethnomusicology* case study (Chapter 3). Music institutions can encourage research into the connections between music and sustainability through PhD study and targeted research grants (Grant, 2016). Managers of musical organisations can investigate the impact of their group on the social sustainability of their local area, as described in the *symphony orchestras and sustainability* case study (Chapter 6). For all these musicians, the material in this book, and the references to further reading, can broaden their views of their professional role and responsibilities, and suggest further ways of addressing problems of sustainability.

While many professional groups and individual musicians have included sustainability as part of their goals, groups formed by newly graduated musicians are often in the forefront of such efforts. Comprising mostly younger musicians, they may be more idealistic and more keenly aware of the problems, and they may feel that they have less to lose than more recognised groups. They may need to utilise unconventional artistic approaches to compete with established performers to break into the music professional scene. There have been several examples from the Sydney Conservatorium of Music, and other music schools will undoubtedly have their own. The Dreambox Collective, discussed in the *composition* case study (Chapter 4), is such a group of performers, a musician and artist collective 'playing at the intersections of musical worlds and social justice' (www.thedreambox collective.com/) with the specific aim of creating performances that highlight the climate emergency and social injustices. In the field of popular music, Lime Cordiale's recent album *14 Steps to a Better You* was mentioned in the case study of *musical creolisation* (Chapter 7). The band sings about their generation's concerns, personal and sometimes global as in the case of *Addicted to the Sunshine*, which takes aim at people who just sit by and do nothing to help stop climate change.

Musicians in community settings, professional or otherwise, have a critical role to play for sustainability. They are embedded in local activity, have local knowledge, and know the needs and culture of the immediate community. Community musicians have a societal reach that is usually very different from formal ensembles. They are active at community celebrations such as weddings, funerals, and parties, and many participate for the simple joy of playing music together. Community music makers take for their artistic topics conditions that are of immediate concern to the local group – overcrowding from new buildings, insufficient public transport, establishment of community gardens. Taken as a whole, they create a cultural vibrancy that reflects the concerns and joys of their community. The participants and their audience make a contribution towards social sustainability, as discussed in the *participatory music* case study (Chapter 6). Involvement (at any age) in community music-making ensures that knowledge is passed between participants, and stories about the community are shared as *intangible cultural heritage*, as discussed in the case study in Chapter 3. From an Indigenous viewpoint, all music can be viewed as community music, encapsulating the culture and knowledge of the whole community, as described in the *Australian Indigenous music* case study in Chapter 7.

It should not be forgotten that many music professionals include teaching as part of their professional work. They have an important role in educating the next generation of musicians in all aspects of music, using as much as possible a broad curriculum that situates music as an approach to life and highlights its interactions with areas of social and environmental concern, such as sustainability.

Conclusion – Sustainability is a Central Concept in Music

Music is an embodied part of human living, the rhythm and sound of our lives. It is a social and cultural practice that communicates on an essential and personal level. As it is imbued with the values and ideas of composers, performers, and participants, it is an ideal medium to deal with broader issues of the world. Sustainability is a sensitising idea at the heart of creative and cultural practice, and so a natural focus for musicians and other artists. Sustainability – although not using this specific term – has always been a consideration for humanity. The oldest-known Middle English part song, the 13th-century rota 'Sumer is Icumen In', focuses on knowledge of the seasons, agriculture, and animal husbandry represented in a joyful six-part round. Understanding the world we live in, and acting accordingly, is integral to our relationship with it. Using music to follow the cycles of the natural world is a subtle means of educating people into the ideas of sustainability.

As explored in Chapter 1, music represents a distinct form of knowledge as it engages with the aesthetic and creative aspects of life, using emotional

Conclusion   95

as well as intellectual approaches. Kagan and Kirchberg (2016) argue that education in music can develop and foster an awareness of the complexity of the natural environment, or as they refer to it, the 'musical aesthetics of complexity' (p. 1493). The practice of music provides an experience of complexity that can be applied to multidimensional problems. A person with highly developed musical skills is already attuned to the thinking that is needed to address the complex problems of sustainability. Røyseng (2019) notes that musicians (and artists in general) have strong potential for economic contribution towards the cultural and creative industries. However, many artists see the social contract as focusing on their critique of society and their role in envisioning alternative futures. It seems that in the context of sustainability, particularly environmental sustainability, this will be the greatest contribution of music, not only socially but even economically.

For millennia, Australian Indigenous communities have not made a distinction between knowledge, music, dance, and symbol. These arts are an essential part of the community's being and knowing. Some areas of knowledge are for everyone in a community and shared widely. Other areas of knowledge are sacred, as the environmental resource is also sacred, and can be shared with others when the custodian decides that it is needed. Complex social structures surround the giving and receiving of knowledge, and the connecting of groups of people. First Nations' knowledge represented through music and arts provides an important example of how knowledge about the world can be experienced by a community, and represents a significant ICH. Australian Indigenous communities' songs and dances are often about the relationship between people and the physical world. We believe that this form of musical education could be a powerful way of developing further understanding of sustainability in the contemporary global community.

References

Allen, A. (2016). New directions: Ecological imaginations, soundscapes, and Italian opera. In A. Allen & K. Dawe (Eds.), *Current directions in ecomusicology: Music, culture, nature* (pp. 273–286). New York: Routledge.

Allen, A., & Dawe, K. (2016). *Current directions in ecomusicology: Music, culture, nature.* New York: Routledge.

Angeler, D. (2016). Heavy metal music meets complexity and sustainability science. *SpringerPlus, 5*, 1637. Retrieved from https://springerplus.springeropen.com/articles/10.1186/s40064-016-3288-9

Banks, J., & Lefeber, M. (2018). A mechanical source of Turkish music from 18th-century London. *Early Music, 46*(2), 299–317.

Barker, S. (2021). Road, pendulum, coil. In A. Reid, N. Peres da Costa, & J. Carrigan (Eds.), *Creative research in music: Informed practice, innovation and transcendence* (pp. 201–213). London: Routledge.

Batt-Rawden, K., & Andersen, S. (2020). "Singing has empowered, enchanted and enthralled me" – choirs for wellbeing? *Health Promotion International, 35*, 140–150.

Bennett, D., Coffey, J., Fitzgerald, S., Petocz, P., & Rainnie, A. (2014). Looking inside the portfolio to understand the work of creative workers: A study of creatives in Perth. In G. Hearn, R. Bridgstock, B. Goldsmith, & J. Rodgers (Eds.), *Creative work beyond the creative industries: Innovation, employment and education* (pp. 158–174). Cheltenham, UK: Edward Elgar.

Bennett, D., Reid, A., & Petocz, P. (2014). Creative workers' views on cultural heritage and sustainability. *Journal of Aesthetics and Culture, 6*, 1–13. doi:10.3402/jac.v6.24476

Blackham, A. (2015). Managing without default retirement in universities: A comparative picture from Australia. *Legal Studies, 35*(3), 502–531.

Blackham, A. (2020). Unpacking precarious academic work in legal education. *The Law Teacher, 54*(3), 426–442.

Bottrill, C., & Tsiarta, C. (2010). *Moving arts – managing the carbon impacts of our touring. Vol. 2: Orchestras.* London: Julie's Bicycle. Retrieved from www.juliesbicycle.com

References

Bowden, J., & Green, P. (Eds.). (2005). *Doing developmental phenomenography*. Melbourne: RMIT University Press.

Boyle, A., & Waterman, E. (2016). The ecology of musical performance: Towards a robust methodology. In A. Allen & K. Dawe (Eds.), *Current directions in ecomusicology: Music, culture, nature* (pp. 25–39). New York: Routledge.

Bracknell, C. (2017). Conceptualizing Noongar song. *2017 Yearbook for Traditional Music, 49*, 92–113.

Bradshaw, M. (2019, November 25). *Elbphilharmonie Orchestra adapts Vivaldi's Four Seasons to reflect climate change*. Rhinegold Publishing. Retrieved from www.rhinegold.co.uk/classical_music/elbphilharmonie-orchestra-adapts-vivaldis-four-seasons-to-reflect-climate-change/

Brennan, M., & Devine, K. (2020). The cost of music. *Popular Music, 39*(1), 43–65.

Campbell, G. (2013). Sustaining Tiwi song practice through Kulama. *Musicology Australia, 35*(2), 237–252.

Chan, C. (2018). Sustainability of indigenous folk tales, music and cultural heritage through innovation. *Journal of Cultural Heritage Management and Sustainable Development, 8*(3), 342–361.

Chan, C., & Saidon, Z. (2017). Advocating contemporary traditional indigenous Semai music through an exploration of youth interest. *International Journal of Academic Research in Business and Social Sciences, 7*(7).

Cook, S. (1995). "Yue Ji" – record of music: Introduction, translation, notes, and commentary. *Asian Music, 26*(2), 1–96.

Curtis, S. (2016). Music therapy for women who have experienced domestic violence. In J. Edwards (Ed.), *The Oxford handbook of music therapy* (pp. 289–298). Oxford: Oxford University Press.

Dalton, D. (2018). *The hometown advantage: Community engagement for professional orchestra sustainability in the U.S.* (Master's thesis), American University, Washington, DC. Retrieved from https://search.proquest.com/docview/2038384676?pq-origsite=gscholar&fromopenview=true

Dawe, K. (2016). Materials matter: Towards a political ecology of music instrument making. In A. Allen & K. Dawe (Eds.), *Current directions in ecomusicology: Music, culture, nature* (pp. 109–121). New York: Routledge.

Dessein, J., Soini, K., Fairclough, G., & Horlings, L. (Eds.). (2015). *Culture in, for and as sustainable development: Conclusions from the COST action IS1007 investigating cultural sustainability*. University of Jyväskylä. Retrieved from www.culturalsustainability.eu/conclusions.pdf

D'Evelyn, C. (2018). Grasping intangible heritage and reimagining Inner Mongolia: Folk-artist albums and a new logic for musical representation in China. *Journal of Folklore Research, 55*(1), 21–48.

Devine, K. (2019). *Decomposed: The political ecology of music*. Cambridge, MA: MIT Press.

Duxbury, N., & Jeannotte, M. (2013). The role of cultural resources in community sustainability: Linking concepts to practice and planning. *The International Journal of Sustainability Policy and Practice, 8*(4), 133–144.

References

Duxbury, N., Kangas, A., & De Beukelaer, C. (2017). Cultural policies for sustainable development: Four strategic paths. *International Journal of Cultural Policy*, *23*(2), 214–230.

Edwards, J. (2016). *The Oxford handbook of music therapy*. Oxford: Oxford University Press.

Ford, F. (2018, March). Songlines on screen: Naina Sen's "The Song Keepers" and Aboriginal histories. *Metro Magazine: Media and Education Magazine*, *195*, 78–84.

Gelbart, M. (2018). Scale. In A. Rehding & S. Rings (Eds.), *The Oxford handbook of critical concepts in music theory* (pp. 78–106). Oxford: Oxford University Press.

Gillespie, K. (2013). Ethnomusicology and the mining industry: A case study from Lihir, Papua New Guinea. *Musicology Australia*, *35*(2), 178–190.

Grant, C. (2016). Music sustainability strategies and interventions. In H. Schippers & C. Grant (Eds.), *Sustainable futures for music cultures: An ecological perspective* (pp. 19–42). Oxford: Oxford University Press.

Hannan, M. (2012). Reflections on the protean music career. In D. Bennett (Ed.), *Life in the real world: How to make music graduates employable* (Ch. 8, pp. 125–143). Champagne, IL: Common Ground.

Haslbeck, F. (2012). Music therapy for premature infants and their parents: An integrative review. *Nordic Journal of Music Therapy*, *21*(3), 203–226.

Hesser, B., & Bartleet, B. (2020). *Music as a Global Resource: Solutions for cultural, social, health, educational, environmental, and economic issues* (5th Ed.). Music as a Global Resource, New York. Retrieved from https://www.musicasaglobalresource.org/2020compendium

Higgins, N. (2020). Songlines and land claims; space and place. *International Journal for the Semiotics of Law*. doi:10.1007/s11196-020-09748-z

Hu, Z. (Lester). (2019). *From ut re mi to fourteen-tone temperament: The global acoustemologies of an early modern Chinese tuning reform* (Ph.D. thesis), The University of Chicago. Retrieved from https://search.proquest.com/docview/2273835354

Hugo, G. (2005). Demographic trends in Australia's academic workforce. *Journal of Higher Education Policy and Management*, *27*(3), 327–343.

International Council for Traditional Music (2020). *ICTM study group on applied ethnomusicology*. Retrieved from www.ictmusic.org/group/applied-ethnomusicology

Isar, Y. (2017). "Culture", "sustainable development" and cultural policy: A contrarian view. *International Journal of Cultural Policy*, *23*(2), 148–158.

James, D. (2013). Signposted by song: Cultural routes of the Australian desert. *Historic Environment*, *25*(3), 30–42.

Jowett, B. (Trans.). (2017). *The Republic of Plato*. Project Gutenberg. Retrieved from www.gutenberg.org/files/55201/55201-h/55201-h.htm

Kagan, S., & Kirchberg, V. (2016). Music and sustainability: Organizational cultures towards creative resilience – a review. *Journal of Cleaner Production*, *135*, 1487–1502.

Kahn, R. (2013). Environmental activism in music. In J. Edmondson (Ed.), *Music in American life: An encyclopedia of the songs, styles, stars, and stories that shaped our culture* (pp. 412–417). Santa Barbara, CA: ABC-CLIO.

References

Kangas, A., Duxbury, N., & De Beukelaer, C. (2017). Introduction: Cultural policies for sustainable development. *International Journal of Cultural Policy*, *23*(2), 129–132.

Kindvall, L. (2019). *Making art for sustainability?* (Master's thesis), Uppsala University, Sweden. Retrieved from www.diva-portal.org/smash/get/diva2:1327145/FULLTEXT01.pdf

Lee, R. (2009). Protest music as alternative media during the Vietnam war era. In P. Haridakis, B. Hugenberg, & S. Wearden (Eds.), *War and the media: Essays on news reporting, propaganda and popular culture* (pp. 24–40). Jefferson, NC: McFarland & Company.

Leeson, J. (2020, July 14). Review: Lime Cordiale – 14 Steps To A Better You. *Canberra Times*. Retrieved from www.canberratimes.com.au/story/6833384/lime-cordiale-sweet-pop-mix-slides-down-easily/?cs=14243

Lehmberg, L., & Fung, C. (2010). Benefits of music participation for senior citizens: A review of the literature. *Music Education Research International*, *4*, 19–30. Retrieved from http://cmer.arts.usf.edu/content/articlefiles/3122-meri04pp.19-30.pdf

Lim, L. (2021). How to make a woodblock sing: Artistic research as an art of attentiveness. In A. Reid, N. Peres da Costa, & J. Carrigan (Eds.), *Creative research in music: Informed practice, innovation and transcendence* (pp. 110–121). New York: Routledge.

Live Music Office (2014). *The economic and cultural value of live music in Australia*. University of Tasmania. Retrieved from https://livemusicoffice.com.au/wp-content/uploads/2015/08/LiveMusic-report-FINAL.pdf

Loughland, T., Reid, A., & Petocz, P. (2002). Young people's conceptions of environment: A phenomenographic analysis. *Environmental Education Research*, *8*(2), 187–197.

Luo, M. (2018). Cultural policy and revolutionary music during China's Cultural Revolution: The case of the Shanghai Symphony Orchestra. *International Journal of Cultural Policy*, *24*(4), 431–450. Retrieved from www.tandfonline.com/doi/full/10.1080/10286632.2016.1219351

Lynch, T. (2020). "Tuning the lyre, tuning the soul": Harmonia, justice and the kosmos of the soul in Plato's Republic and Timaeus. *Greek and Roman Musical Studies*, *8*, 111–155.

Mack, D. (2021). Remarks on music in Indonesia. In A. Reid, N. Peres da Costa, & J. Carrigan (Eds.), *Creative research in music: Informed practice, innovation and transcendence* (pp. 141–150). London: Routledge.

Maddox, A. (2017). J.S. Bach's *St Matthew Passion* and intellectual history. *Intellectual History Review*, *27*(3), 333–349.

Marton, F., & Booth, S. (1997). *Learning and awareness*. Mahwah, NJ: Lawrence Erlbaum.

Matsunobu, K. (2013). Instrument-making as music-making: An ethnographic study of *shakuhachi* students' learning experiences. *International Journal of Music Education*, *31*(2). doi:10.1177/0255761413486858

Matyakubov, O. (1993). A traditional musician in modern society: A case study of Turgun Alimatov's art. *Yearbook of Traditional Music*, *25*, 60–66. Retrieved from www.jstor.org/stable/768684

References

McBride, J., & Tlusty, T. (2020). *Cross-cultural data shows musical scales evolved to maximise imperfect fifths*. E-print. Retrieved from https://arxiv.org/pdf/1906.06171.pdf

McConnell, T., & Porter, S. (2017). Music therapy for palliative care: A realist review. *Palliative and Supportive Care, 15*(4), 454–464.

McLellan, B., Corder, G., Golev, A., & Ali, S. (2014). Sustainability of the rare earths industry. *Procedia Environmental Sciences, 20*, 280–287.

McPherson, A. (2021, January 13). Review: The [Uncertain] Four Seasons. *Limelight*. Retrieved from www.limelightmagazine.com.au/reviews/the-uncertain-four-seasons-sydney-symphony-orchestra-sydney-festival/

Music Australia (2016). *National Contemporary Music Plan*. Retrieved from https://musicaustralia.org.au/wp-content/uploads/2016/08/National-Contemporary-Music-Plan-Aug-2016-final.pdf

Perry, L., & Holt, L. (2018). Searching for the Songlines of Aboriginal education and culture within Australian higher education. *Australian Educational Researcher, 45*, 343–361. Retrieved from https://link.springer.com/article/10.1007/s13384-017-0251-x

Petocz, P., & Reid, A. (2003). What on earth is sustainability in mathematics? *New Zealand Journal of Mathematics, 32*(Suppl.), 135–144.

Petocz, P., Reid, A., & Bennett, D. (2014). The music workforce, cultural heritage and sustainability. *International Journal of Culture and Creative Industries, 1*(2), 4–16.

Petocz, P., Reid, A., & Loughland, T. (2003). *The importance of adults' conceptions of the environment for education* (P. L. Jeffery, Compiled). Australian Association for Research in Education 2003 Conference Papers, AARE, Melbourne. Retrieved from www.aare.edu.au/data/publications/2003/pet03250.pdf

Ramnarine, T. (2011). The orchestration of civil society: Community and conscience in symphony orchestras. *Ethnomusicology Forum, 20*(3), 327–351. doi:10.1080/17411912.2011.638515

Rees, H. (2016). Environmental crisis, culture loss, and a new musical aesthetic: China's "Original Ecology Folksongs" in theory and practice. *Ethnomusicology, 60*(1), 53–88.

Reid, A., Peres Da Costa, N., & Carrigan, J. (Eds.). (2021). *Creative research in music: Informed practice, innovation and transcendence*. New York: Routledge.

Reid, A., & Petocz, P. (2005). What is sustainability in the arts? In *Enhancing curricula: Towards the scholarship of teaching in art, design and communication in higher education* (pp. 345–361). London: Centre for Learning and Teaching in Art & Design, University of the Arts London.

Reid, A., & Petocz, P. (2006). University lecturers' understanding of sustainability. *Higher Education, 51*(1), 105–123.

Reid, A., & Petocz, P. (2007). Internationalisation as an orientation for learning in mathematics. In B. Atweh, H. Forgasz, & B. Nebres (Eds.), *Internationalisation and globalisation in mathematics and science education* (pp. 247–267). Dordrecht, The Netherlands: Springer.

References

Reid, A., Petocz, P., & Taylor, P. (2009). Business students' conceptions of sustainability. *Sustainability*, *1*(3), 662–673. Retrieved from www.mdpi.com/2071-1050/1/3/662

Røyseng, S. (2019). The social contract of artists in the era of cultural industries. *International Journal of Cultural Policy*, *25*(2), 154–170.

Ryan, R. (2016). No tree – no leaf: Applying resilience theory to eucalypt-derived musical traditions. In A. Allen & K. Dawe (Eds.), *Current directions in ecomusicology: Music, culture, nature* (pp. 57–68). New York: Routledge.

Saarikallio, S., Stensaeth, K., Horwitz, E., Ekholm, O., & Bonde, L. (2020). Music as a resource for psychological health for music professionals: A Nordic survey. *Nordic Journal of Arts, Culture and Health*, *2*(1), 38–50.

Schröder, A. (2018). Aesthetic strategies to explore beyond the models of sustainable development: An analysis of Lisa Simpson's *Musical Sewing*. *Sustainable Development*, *26*(2), 182–189. doi:10.1002/sd.1729

Shevock, D. (2015). The possibility of eco-literate music pedagogy. *Topics for Music Education Praxis*, *1*, 1–23. Retrieved from http://topics.maydaygroup.org/articles/2015/Shevock2015.pdf

Shevock, D. (2018). *Eco-literate music pedagogy*. New York: Routledge.

Simonett, H. (2016). Of human and non-human birds: Indigenous music making and sentient ecology in Northwestern Mexico. In A. Allen & K. Dawe (Eds.), *Current directions in ecomusicology: Music, culture, nature* (pp. 99–108). New York: Routledge.

Soini, K., & Dessein, J. (2016). Culture-sustainability relation: Towards a conceptual framework. *Sustainability*, *8*(2), 167. Retrieved from www.mdpi.com/2071-1050/8/2/167

Spohr, A. (2012). "This charming invention created by the King" – Christian IV and his invisible music. *Danish Yearbook of Musicology*, *39*, 13–33. Retrieved from www.dym.dk/dym_pdf_files/volume_39/volume_39_013_033.pdf

Stefano, M., & Murphy, C. (2016). "We can always go back home": Critical lessons in helping to safeguard and promote the Singing and Praying Bands living tradition. *International Journal of Heritage Studies*, *22*(8), 607–621.

Suárez, R., Alonso, A., & Sendra, J. (2015). Intangible cultural heritage: The sound of the Romanesque cathedral of Santiago de Compostela. *Journal of Cultural Heritage*, *16*(2), 239–243. doi:10.1016/j.culher.2014.05.008

Taylor, P. (2016). Why is a STEAM curriculum perspective crucial to the 21st century? Australian Council for Educational Research. Retrieved from https://research.acer.edu.au/research_conference/RC2016/9august/6/

Throsby, D. (2008). Modelling the cultural industries. *International Journal of Cultural Policy*, *14*(3), 217–232.

Throsby, D. (2017). Culturally sustainable development: Theoretical concept or practical policy instrument? *International Journal of Cultural Policy*, *23*(2), 133–147.

Throsby, D. (2020). Cultural statistics. In R. Towse & T. Hernández (Eds.), *Handbook of cultural economics* (3rd ed., pp. 197–205). Cheltenham, UK: Edward Elgar.

Thwink.org (2014). *Sustainability*. Retrieved from www.thwink.org/sustain/glossary/Sustainability.htm

Titon, J. (2009). Music and sustainability: An ecological viewpoint. *The World of Music*, *51*(1), 119–137.

Titon, J. (2013). The nature of ecomusicology. *Música e Cultura: Revista da ABET*, *8*(1), 8–18. Retrieved from www.abet.mus.br/musicaecultura/#vol08

Titon, J. (2016). Why Thoreau? In A. Allen & K. Dawe (Eds.), *Current directions in ecomusicology: Music, culture, nature* (pp. 69–79). New York: Routledge.

Titon, J. (2020). *Towards a sound ecology: New and selected essays*. Bloomington: Indiana University Press.

Turino, T. (2009). Four fields of music making and sustainable living. *The World of Music: Music and Sustainability*, *51*(1), 95–117.

UIS (UNESCO Institute of Statistics) (2009). *The 2009 UNESCO framework for cultural statistics (FCS)*. Retrieved from http://uis.unesco.org/sites/default/files/documents/unesco-framework-for-cultural-statistics-2009-en_0.pdf

UNESCO (2003). *Text of the Convention for the Safeguarding of the Intangible cultural Heritage*. Retrieved from https://ich.unesco.org/en/convention

UNESCO (2018). *Sustainable development: World heritage and sustainable development*. Retrieved from http://whc.unesco.org/en/sustainabledevelopment/

United Nations (1987). *Report of the World Commission on Environment and Development: Our Common Future*. Retrieved from www.un-documents.net/our-common-future.pdf

United Nations (2002). *Report of the World Summit on Sustainable Development*. Retrieved from www.un-documents.net/aconf199-20.pdf

United Nations (2015). *Transforming our World: The 2030 Agenda for Sustainable Development*. Retrieved from https://sustainabledevelopment.un.org/post2015/transformingourworld/publication

University of Cambridge (2019). *Retirement policy*. Retrieved from www.hr.admin.cam.ac.uk/policies-procedures/1-retirement-policy

Waren, W. (2012). Theories of the Singing Revolution: An historical analysis of the role of music in the Estonian independence movement. *International Review of the Aesthetics and Sociology of Music*, *43*(2), 439–451.

Wilson, O. (2013). Popular music as local culture: An ethnographic study of the album *Matha Wa!* by the band Paramana Strangers from Papua New Guinea. *Musicology Australia*, *35*(2), 253–267.

Windsor, L. (2016). Nature and culture, noise and music, perception and action. In A. Allen & K. Dawe (Eds.), *Current directions in ecomusicology: Music, culture, nature* (pp. 98–108). New York: Routledge.

Withers, D. (2015). Intangible cultural heritage and the women's liberation music archive. In S. Cohen, R. Knifton, M. Leonard, & L. Roberts (Eds.), *Sites of popular music heritage: Memories, histories, places* (pp. 125–141). London: Routledge.

Wolcott, S. (2016). The role of music in the transition towards a culture of sustainability. *Empowering Sustainability International Journal*, *3*(1), 1–20. Retrieved from https://escholarship.org/uc/item/4vx624mc#main

Wong, C. F. (2019). "Original ecology" style of China's minority performing arts; examples from Uyghur music. In K. W. Lo & J. Yeung (Eds.), *Chinese *shock of the anthropocene: Image, music and text in the age of climate change* (pp. 203–223). Singapore: Palgrave Macmillan.

Yeadon, D. (2021). Historically informed performance and group-learning pedagogy in a tertiary music ensemble. In A. Reid, N. Peres Da Costa, & J. Carrigan (Eds.), *Creative research in music: Informed practice, innovation and transcendence* (pp. 43–52). London: Routledge.

Zarate, R. (2016). The social architecture of anxiety and potential role of music therapy. *Voices: A World Forum for Music Therapy*, *16*(1). Retrieved from https://voices.no/index.php/voices/article/view/2328/2083

Index

acoustic archaeology 34
analogy 4, 9, 11, 79
Analogy 4,
Australian Chamber Orchestra 46, 63

baby boomers 58
Bach 10, 11, 36, 77
Bolivia 72, 75, 76
broad curriculum 85, 86, 94
Brundtland 13, 14
Bunuba 78
business skills 57

capstone project 57, 92
casualisation 59
China 3, 26, 29, 30, 31, 44, 70, 91
Christian IV 43, 44
climate change 5, 10, 38, 42, 45, 71, 79, 81, 93
Coldplay 45
community choir 66
community music 66, 94
compact disc 51
conductor 63
Confucius 3
cost of music 49, 50, 52, 89
Covid-19 42, 45, 60, 66, 75, 79
Creative Trident 56
creolisation 25, 72, 76–79, 91, 93
cultural industries 50, 53–55
cultural production chain 54

Decade of Education for Sustainable Development 20, 86
didjeridu 39, 78

Dowling Songbook 74
download 51
Dreambox Collective 43, 57, 93

early music 3, 12, 25, 39, 72–76, 91
ecomusicology 31, 38, 46–48, 87, 91
Ensemble Apex 46, 57
ethnomusicology 26–29, 86, 88, 91, 93

feminist 34, 69
Florilegium 75, 76
four pillars 15–17, 72, 73, 84

gamelan 35, 36, 63, 91
Garma Festival 81
greenhouse gas 45, 53

Harmony of the Spheres 5–7, 9
harpsichord 39
heavy metal 10
historically informed performance/practice 74
Homer 6, 8

Indigenous music 73, 79–81, 94
Indonesia 88, 91
intangible cultural heritage 19, 20, 25–29, 32, 34, 88, 94, 95
inter-generational equity 58
Isidore of Seville 6
ivory 1, 39, 40, 74, 75

Jandamarra 78, 91
jazz 56, 57, 73, 78, 79, 91
Julie's Bicycle 45

kamancha 33
Kepler, Johannes 6
khöömei 32
Kronos Quartet 44

Ladysmith Black Mambazo 78
Lime Cordiale 77, 93
LP album 51, 52

Mahabharata 8
Massive Attack 45
metaphor 7, 9, 11, 16, 62–64
modes 6, 35, 36
morin huur 31
Mozart 77
Musical Sewing 10
music pedagogy 48, 87
music therapy 61, 67–69
myth 7, 9, 11

narrow curriculum 85, 90
National Institute of Dramatic Art 46
Noongar 8, 82

original ecology folksong 26, 27, 29–31

Paradisec 81
participatory music 66, 89, 94
participatory performance 66
Perentie Lizard 8
phenomenography 21
Pinchgut Opera 75
Plato 5, 6
portfolio career 56
protean 56, 97
Pythagoras 5, 34

Rameau 77
rare earth 40
recordings 25, 42, 51, 52, 57, 65, 68, 75, 79–81

retirement age 50, 58, 59
revolutionary change 69
Ripple Effect Band 81

scale 4, 26, 34–36
Seven Sisters 8
shakuhachi 40
Singing Revolution 71
social contract 92, 95
societal change 62, 69
Socrates 5
Songlines 8, 82
Stolen Generations 80
streaming 49, 51, 52, 54, 77
studio audio art 65
Sustainable Development Goals 16, 17, 19
Sydney Chamber Opera 42, 64
Sydney Conservatorium of Music 12, 42–44, 46, 57, 64, 78, 91, 93
Sydney Symphony Orchestra 42, 44
symphony orchestra 61–64

temperament 35, 36
three pillars 2, 14, 15, 37, 49, 61
Tjuku pil7–11

Uluru Statement 80
United Nations 13, 14, 16, 17, 20, 32, 86
Uyghur 30, 31

Vivaldi 41, 42, 75, 77

wanji-wanji 81
Women's Liberation Music Archive 34
Woodstock 70

Yolngu 8, 81
Yothu Yindi 81
Yueji 3, 5, 9

Taylor & Francis eBooks

www.taylorfrancis.com

A single destination for eBooks from Taylor & Francis with increased functionality and an improved user experience to meet the needs of our customers.

90,000+ eBooks of award-winning academic content in Humanities, Social Science, Science, Technology, Engineering, and Medical written by a global network of editors and authors.

TAYLOR & FRANCIS EBOOKS OFFERS:

- A streamlined experience for our library customers
- A single point of discovery for all of our eBook content
- Improved search and discovery of content at both book and chapter level

REQUEST A FREE TRIAL
support@taylorfrancis.com

For Product Safety Concerns and Information please contact our EU representative GPSR@taylorandfrancis.com
Taylor & Francis Verlag GmbH, Kaufingerstraße 24, 80331 München, Germany

www.ingramcontent.com/pod-product-compliance
Lightning Source LLC
Chambersburg PA
CBHW051756230426
43670CB00012B/2316